Day Paddling Florida's 10,000 Islands and Big Cypress Swamp

Sunrise over 10,000 Islands

Day Paddling Florida's 10,000 Islands and Big Cypress Swamp

Jeff Ripple

BACK COUNTRY

BACKCOUNTRY GUIDES
WOODSTOCK, VERMONT

ISBN 0-88150-564-1

Cover and interior design by Faith Hague
Composition by Chelsea Cloeter
Cover & interior photographs by the author
Maps by Paul Woodward, © 2003 The Countryman Press

Published by Backcountry Guides,
a division of The Countryman Press,
P.O. Box 748, Woodstock, Vermont 05091

Distributed by W.W. Norton & Company, Inc.,
500 Fifth Avenue, New York, NY 10110

Printed in the United States of America

10 9 8 7 6 5 4 3 2

Dedicated to Clyde and Niki Butcher,
and to the memory of Oscar Thompson, who loved these islands.

Contents

Acknowledgments

I would like to thank the following individuals and agencies for their assistance in preparing this book: Sandy and David Herraden for the great adventures with NALT-Everglades Eco-Adventures and tasty meals at the Ghost Orchid Grill, as well as the rest of the hard-working staff at the Ivey House; Clyde and Niki Butcher (for everything); Paul Kubilis (mapping and patient, albeit unsuccessful in my case, tutor of GIS systems); Fakahatchee Strand State Preserve, in particular Mike Owen; Big Cypress National Preserve, in particular Sandy Snell Dolbert, Deb Jansen, Frank Partridge, and Carol Clark; Steve Dolbert; Everglades National Park, Gulf Coast Ranger Station; Rookery Bay National Estuarine Research Reserve; Collier-Seminole State Park; 10,000 Islands National Wildlife Refuge; Frank Corso, artist, paddling companion, and model for the cover photo; and my mom, Judy Ripple. I also am grateful to Renée Ripple, who typed most of the transcriptions of my taped notes from which I based my route descriptions. I would also like to thank Kermit Hummel of Countryman Press for his patience and gentle insistence that I do this book.

Introduction

"10,000 Islands is a region of mystery and loneliness; gloomy, monotonous, weird and strange, yet possessing a decided fascination. To the casual stranger each and every part of the region looks exactly like all the rest; each islet and water passage seems but the counterpart of the hundreds of others. Even those who long have lived within this region and are familiar with its tortuous channels often get lost." So wrote naturalist Charles Torrey Simpson to sum up his impression of the islands in his classic *In Lower Florida Wilds*, published in 1921. 10,000 Islands is a misnomer of sorts; there aren't really that many islands along this stretch of southwest Florida coastline from Marco Island to Cape Sable, but to anyone who has traveled by boat among the countless islands, channels, and creeks, it seems that way.

The 10,000 Islands offer much to paddlers, including backcountry paddling, sandy beaches, birding, wildlife watching, and fishing. Most guidebooks devoted to paddlers and covering Everglades National Park or southern Florida focus on overnight trips and paddling the Wilderness Waterway. This book is different. All of the routes covered in this guide can be done in a day and are 14 miles in length or less. Several trips are 5 miles long or less. Most are loop trips, but some may require you to make shuttle arrangements. I have been paddling this region for nearly 20 years, mostly on day trips and short overnight trips. The possibilities for exploration and discovery remain limitless to me and I think they will be for you too. The islands can be formidable to navigate, but my hope is that this guide will provide enough direction for you to plan a paddling adventure without unpleasant surprises. All of these routes can be paddled in a canoe or a kayak, but on certain routes

I make recommendations regarding boat length.

You can also extend your range of exploration in the 10,000 Islands by embarking on what are called skiff tours. Kayaks are loaded onto a skiff that gets you close to your destination. You off-load the kayaks, explore for three or four hours, and then return to the boat for the trip back to town. Skiff tours solve the often asked question by clients of kayak guides toward the end of a day on the water: "Where is the motor?" You can hire a service that runs trips like these or use your own skiff and kayaks. Suggested destinations for this type of trip include New River, New Turkey Key, and the Ferguson River.

As you paddle the routes in this book, you will notice that very few of them are posted with markers. Among Everglades National Park, Big Cypress National Preserve, Fakahatchee Strand State Preserve, and Collier-Seminole State Park, there are only a handful of established, marked trails. They are Sandfly Island, Turner River, Left-Hand Turner River, Halfway Creek, East River, and Blackwater River. There is a park map available for each of these. The route I call Halfway Creek/Barron River Loop is now a marked route in the Big Cypress National Preserve, although I have not yet paddled it with the new marker system. In light of the scarcity of marked trails, it is imperative you carry a chart and compass and know how to use them. One visitor after a cruise to the 10,000 Islands in 1885 remarked in reference to available maps of the area "for general outline they were superb, but for particulars all of them were signal failures." Technology has improved since 1885 and the maps in this guide will not be *signal failures,* but do not rely on them as your sole source of navigation and I advise you that the directions for these routes are not bombproof. I created most of the routes by poring over maps and tracing wriggling creeks through interesting areas and over an appropriate distance, not knowing if they truly went where they promised until I actually got on the water and paddled them. Considering the region, it goes without saying that these are routes that were not unerringly traveled, but I have personally covered every inch of them.

One of the nice things about the 10,000 Islands is that there are so many islands, creeks, and mangrove tunnels and no one has bothered

Mangroves

The 10,000 Islands and southern Everglades comprise the largest mangrove forest in the United States. The red mangrove *(Rhizophora mangle)*, black mangrove *(Avicennia germinans)*, and the white mangrove *(Laguncularia racemosa)* are the only mangroves found in Florida. Red mangroves are easy to identify by their distinctive arching prop roots and curtain-like veils of drop roots hanging from upper limbs. You can distinguish black mangroves by the snorkel-like pneumatophores that radiate several feet from the base of the tree. White mangroves are the least common and found farthest back in the mangrove fringe. Apparently they too develop pneumatophores, although they are much sparser than those of black mangroves and look more like cypress knees. White mangroves should not be confused with buttonwood trees, which are not true mangroves but closely resemble them and are common in south Florida mangrove forests. They prefer water that is less salty and are named for the button-like seed and spray of tiny flowers. None of Florida's mangroves produce annual tree rings like northern deciduous trees.

Mangroves are tropical intertidal evergreen plants grouped by their common morphological features and adaptive mechanisms rather than their membership in any one particular taxonomic genus or family. Fossil evidence suggests that mangroves evolved from freshwater flowering plants about 70 million years ago. They all share highly specialized adaptations, including exposed breathing roots, support roots, salt-excretion and exclusion mechanisms, and viviparous propagules. Mangroves represent more than 60 species from 20 different families of plants that include trees, shrubs, palms, and even ground ferns. About 80 percent of all mangrove species are found in the Indo Pacific, while only 5 percent or so live in the Caribbean, including south Florida.

Mangroves survive in salty soil and water not so much because they need it, but because the salty conditions exclude other plants that would grow faster in freshwater conditions. All mangroves have mechanisms for excluding salt to varying degrees. Black mangroves exclude some salt but get rid of most of the salt in their tissues by secreting it through salt glands and fine hairs on both the top and bottom sides of the leaves. The salt crystallizes on the leaves and then blows away. Red mangroves are more efficient at keeping salt from entering their tissues in the first place. Many mangroves get rid of excess salt by shedding leaves.

Most mangroves produce small white or yellowish flowers that may be pollinated by large moths, bees, and wasps, or even by the wind. Red mangroves are thought to be pollinated mainly by wind because the pollen is powdery and there is no pleasant odor and nectar reward. They may also self-pollinate, although bees seem to like them despite the supposed lack of nectar. Black mangroves are hermaphroditic, meaning both male and female flower types are found on the same tree. Bees pollinate black mangrove flowers, which are fragrant and produce plenty of nectar from glandular hairs on the flower surface.

A mangrove forms a fruit from a pollinated flower and from the fruit a live seedling, called a propagule, emerges. Every flower does not produce a propagule because many succumb to insect and fungus infestations. After several weeks the propagule drops off the tree to float away on the tide. Mangrove propagules can survive from a few months to more than a year floating on the currents. It takes most mangroves 5–15 days after the propagule lodges in suitable sediment to produce a couple of leaves and develop an anchoring root system.

Mangrove forests are considered pioneer communities, establishing tenuous rootholds in areas where other plants have not been able to colonize, such as oyster bars and sandbars. Mangroves were once thought to be land-builders, but now it is known that they respond to accumulation of sediments and changes in shoreline, not cause the changes. They are critical for stabilizing shorelines. Mangroves also help filter harmful sediments before they enter waters near the shore, and they provide shelter for small fish and shellfish among their roots. Gaps in the forest canopy are important for the establishment of new mangroves, and catastrophic events such as hurricanes and occasional freezes actually promote the growth of young mangrove trees, which grow better in bright light rather than under the canopy.

Mangrove leaves are eaten by many insects, such as the common mangrove skipper, and shed a few at a time, which forms the basis for a highly productive chain of life in the 10,000 Island estuaries. Mangroves drop more than three tons of leaves per acre each year, beginning a cycle that starts once the tannins in the leaves have leached into the water (this is what stains the water its reddish hue). Microorganisms attack the leaf and begin to break it down. Bits of leaf matter are consumed by crabs, snails, sea worms, and mullet, which are in turn are eaten by larger fish and animals as diverse as dolphins and egrets.

to name them all. Local folks may have names for some of these places, but they rarely appear on commercially available charts. I like traveling through nameless places, partly for the mystery (I respect a place that can remain nameless in the 21st century) and also because I don't need to waste precious time wondering how the names came to be. For a guidebook author, however, there is a need to describe concisely and precisely how to navigate a route and a dearth of place names on charts poses problems. Assigning places names for convenience sake requires a certain hubris I don't possess, although I did do so for the forks of the Barron River. Therefore, you are on your own to name or not name those islands, bays, and tunnels I describe but allow to remain *nameless*.

A note about powerboats. The 10,000 Islands are notorious for shallow water and famous for sport fishing. You will encounter many powerboats, although I have carefully worked the routes in this guide to avoid popular boating channels as much as possible. If you are paddling on the flats or in a shallow channel on a low tide stage, most skiffs will not come off plane to slow for you because they may run aground. A powerboat draws more water when it is not on plane, and in many places in the 10,000 Islands that makes the difference between it floating and not. When paddling in channels, stay off to one side or paddle just outside the channel. Most boaters are considerate and will slow down when they can if they think their wake will cause problems for you.

When to Paddle

You can paddle in southwest Florida throughout the year. Ice on the water is never a problem, and even in summer, a sea breeze usually stirs the air. Summer paddling is unpopular with most folks, though, for obvious reasons. Daytime temperatures often exceed 90 degrees and thunderstorms occur virtually every day, typically in the afternoon. Don't be surprised by a coastal morning storm as well. Hurricanes are a possibility anytime from June through November.

Count on getting on the water between 6–7 AM (the temperature may already be 80 degrees with 90 percent humidity) and returning before noon. Keep your trip really short and take lots of water. In the mangroves, expect millions of mosquitoes and no-see-ums anxious to be your friend, but what is the Everglades without a bug or two? The benefit of summer paddling is that you're assured of getting a great rate on a motel room and you will probably be the only paddler on the water.

A beautiful day in southwest Florida

Most people paddle in southwest Florida from November through April when the weather is cooler and drier. Average daytime highs range from the mid-70s to low 80s. Low temperatures average in the lower 50s. Relative humidity generally drops as well. However, it can be sunny and 85 degrees one day and 55 degrees with the wind blowing hard from the north the next. Be prepared. Peak paddling season begins in late December between Christmas and New Year's Day and lasts through Easter. Motels and campsites are often full, particularly on weekends and around holidays, such as President's Day or during spring break. Keep this in mind so you can plan ahead with booking motel rooms, campsites, or guided trips.

Canoes and Kayaks

The Big Cypress Swamp and the 10,000 Islands provide beautiful water to paddle in both canoes and kayaks. I spent my first couple of years paddling in the 10,000 Islands in a 14-foot Mohawk kevlar canoe. I love that boat and still have it, although it gets very little time on the water since I began paddling kayaks. I believe that in the 10,000 Islands an average paddler can cover much more water with less effort on a day trip in a kayak than in a canoe, particularly solo. My primary reason for saying this is that wide expanses of open water must be covered in the islands and there is always the possibility of encountering strong wind and tides. Although all of the routes in this guide can be paddled in a canoe or kayak, some of the longer routes should be attempted in canoes only with two strong, experienced paddlers. Solo canoeists should use a boat designed for solo paddling and have experience covering several miles of open water against wind and tide.

Water temperature in the Big Cypress Swamp and 10,000 Islands ranges from relatively warm (depending on where you're from) in the winter to unpleasantly toasty in the summer. As a result, many day-trippers find a sit-on-top kayak is the ideal craft throughout the year. Sit-on-tops come as single- and two-person boats and are made by several manufacturers, including Perception, Wilderness Systems, Necky, and Ocean Kayaks. They are easy to paddle and should you fall off, you just climb back on. Some provide hatches for stowing gear. You are not as cramped as you are in a traditional kayak, particularly if you are taller than 6 feet. Virtually all sit-on-tops are relatively inexpensive. I owned a kayak tour company for several years and used Perception Prisms with great success in all kinds of weather. Sit-on-tops are the most common rental kayaks you'll find.

Traditional *sit inside* kayaks are popular here, too, particularly among people embarking on overnight trips. Day-trippers will find these boats are more comfortable to use than sit-on-tops when the weather is cold and windy, particularly when traversing open water. For folks squeamish about spiders and other creepy crawlers dropping into their laps in mangrove tunnels, a traditional kayak with a skirt may be the answer. If I had to use a single kayak for all my paddling in the 10,000 Islands, I would choose a plastic 15- or 16-foot traditional kayak with a rudder and ample hatches. Such a boat is short enough to paddle through tunnels without clipping roots on corners and long enough, particularly equipped with a rudder, to cover open water and maintain course in a crosswind or tide. A light color like yellow or light gray reflects the sun, keeping the temperature cooler inside the boat. The big hatches allow you to store necessities such as lunch and extra water without having it all piled in your lap and splayed beneath your rigging. The bright color shows up well against the water so that powerboaters can more easily see you (and rescue you if you encounter trouble). Plastic is inexpensive, easy to repair, and stands up the best over the long haul against oysters and blazing sun.

Equipment

Personal Flotation Devices (PFDs) are required equipment. If you don't always wear your PFD, keep it close at hand so you can reach it quickly. Don't bury it in a kayak hatch or under a mountain of gear in the canoe. Not only does a PFD help you float should you fall out of your boat, but it can keep you warm on a cold windy day on the water. You must have one Coast Guard–approved PFD per person per boat or risk being fined by any law enforcement officer you encounter on the water. If you forget and leave yours at home, buy another or find one to rent. It's cheaper than a ticket or losing your life.

Paddles are always a matter of personal preference. Regardless of whether you are paddling a canoe or a kayak, always bring a spare paddle. You are literally *up the creek* if your only paddle should break on an oyster bar, float away as you nap on the beach, or wash out of your hands in heavy waves. Canoeists should bring a long paddle for general use and a short paddle for mangrove tunnels. Kayakers should bring two kayak paddles, in addition to a small canoe paddle for tunnels. I prefer a paddle you can take apart and use offset (feathered), and such a paddle eliminates the need to bring a canoe paddle. You will encounter mud and limestone and oysters, so you want a paddle that is not only light but durable.

Maps and Compasses

There's a laundry list of other items you can bring with you on a day trip, but let me first mention your chart and compass, two more items you should never forget. A common complaint among paddlers new to the 10,000 Islands is that the mangrove islands, bays, and creeks all look the same. All the trees are about the same height and there are few markers and even fewer designated paddling trails. These factors conspire to make navigating difficult to impossible without a compass, a good chart, and a basic understanding of how to use them.

There are several maps of the 10,000 Islands from which to choose. Most do not have the detail you need to follow many of the routes in this guide, particularly those that traverse tidal creeks. I found the single most useful map for the Big Cypress Swamp and 10,000 Islands to be the two-sided Waterproof Chart #40E. It is, as the name implies, waterproof and offers the finest detail (and in many cases the only detail) for all of the routes covered in this guide, with the exception of those originating from Marco Island. It is available at most marinas or by calling International Sailing Supply at 1-800-423-9026 or visiting www.waterproofcharts.com. The Ivey House in Everglades City also carries them.

For the trips from Marco Island, I found the best map for my purposes to be the NOAA Nautical Chart #11430 (Lostmans River to Wiggins Pass), again for the superior detail. It allows you to see holes in which to wriggle a canoe or kayak through that on other charts do not exist. It is not waterproof, so you need to laminate it or protect it in a map case. This map extends to Lostmans River, as does the Waterproof Chart #40E, but the creek detail is not nearly as good. A close second to this chart is the waterproof Pasadena Top Spot Fishing Map. These latter two maps are also available at most marinas. You can also use TerraServer aerial imagery at www.terraserver-usa.com to zoom in for detail of areas inadequate on maps. The Everglades are within 3 degrees of magnetic north, not enough for you to worry about making adjustments on your compass when using the charts.

Any decent fluid-filled compass with a clear base, moveable compass ring, and graduated scale on the base and compass ring will work for your purposes here. Some kayakers use a compass mounted in front of them on their deck. I use a handheld Silva Trekker, which actually provides instructions for using the compass on the packaging. Tie your compass to your clothing or to the boat. If you have never used a compass and map, practice first at home before trying it out on the water. Bring a spare compass in case you lose one.

On the topic of navigating equipment, a Global Positioning Device (GPS) is nice to have and was essential for me to map the routes in this guide. It can add to your feeling of safety. It is not, however, essential navigating equipment, and you should never rely on it as a substitute for a chart and compass. Batteries can and do fail. You will lose satellite signals at one time or another in most of the mangrove tunnels in the 10,000 Islands. I have also lost reception under clear blue sky for brief periods. Unless you purchase a unit with a built-in map, you might be able to navigate from point A to point B, but you won't be certain where you are between the two points; and in the 10,000 Islands, rarely is the distance between point A and point B a straight line with no obstacles. Make sure your unit is a marine model that floats. You will be paddling in salt water.

Emergency Equipment

You may be going on a day tour, but remember the *SS Minnow* and *Gilligan's Island*. Keep the following emergency items in a small, preferably yellow, dry bag, such as the type made by SealLine, so you can bring them with you even if you are renting a boat:

- Emergency whistle
- Spare compass
- Duct tape and silicone marine goop for emergency repairs to your boat
- Line for a towrope or a bow line (keeps your boat from floating away)
- A small first aid kit including waterproof flexible bandages (If you are allergic to insect bites, pack an appropriate antihistamine or other medicine to block serious allergic reaction.)
- NOAA multifrequency weather radio
- Small waterproof flashlight with extra batteries
- Swiss Army knife
- Space blanket (for keeping warm if you get stranded overnight or during a storm)
- Emergency flare
- Energy food bars (in a separate plastic bag inside a dry bag)
- Insect repellant and sunscreen (in a separate heavy-duty

freezer bag so they don't leak all over the inside of the dry bag)
• Lightweight Gore-Tex® windbreaker

Consider also a small can or hand-powered pump (such as those sold in emergency kits for traditional kayaks) with which to bail out water. Other useful but optional equipment includes the following:

• Additional dry bags (I prefer yellow. Dark bags strapped to decks cook what's inside, as do clear bags on sunny days.)
• Binoculars (a small lightweight 8x25 variety for bird-watching or picking out distant navigation markers)
• Field guides to birds, coastal sea life, and plants
• Light spinning or fly tackle and small tackle box
• Needle-nose pliers
• Cell phone (Reception is spotty at best. Do not count on one as your only piece of emergency equipment.)

Clothing and Sun Protection

When choosing what clothing to wear in the Big Cypress Swamp and 10,000 Islands, keep in mind that it should be light-colored and offer protection from the sun. Sunscreen, sunblock for your lips, a wide-brimmed hat or a long-billed flats fishing cap, and polarized sunglasses are also essential. I like to wear a light tan or white long-sleeved fishing shirt such as those made by Columbia, a pair of light-colored cordura nylon long pants that convert to shorts, a wide-brimmed straw hat, and a pair of water sandals (with a pair of old sneakers to wear when walking on oyster bars). This wardrobe is relatively inexpensive, flexible (I can zip off the legs of the pants and roll up the long sleeves), and offers excellent protection against sun and bugs so I don't have to slather a sunscreen/bug dope cocktail all over myself. Shorts and a T-shirt will work fine, too, as long as you use lots of sunscreen. I also bring one or two bandanas that I can soak over the side of the boat and then drape around my neck to offer additional sun protection and cool my neck at the same time. I don't recommend flip flops because mud can easily pull them off your feet and they offer no protection against sharp shells.

Regarding insect protection, I'm a firm believer in covering with clothing rather than bug spray, but if you do use bug repellant, a product with no more than 30 percent deet is sufficient. If you apply it to skin, use it no more than twice a day and wash it off as soon as you are off the water. Avon's Skin-So-Soft is effective against no-see-ums because it forms an oily layer on your skin that these tiny bugs can't get through. It doesn't protect you against mosquitoes, though.

If the weather is cool, dress in layers so you can peel them off or add on as needed. Pack a fleece jacket and wear a windbreaker or Gore-Tex® rain jacket over that for additional layering.

Know Your Physical and Mental Limits

Canoeing and kayaking in southwest Florida is a lot of fun as long as you don't exceed your physical and mental limits. For example, if you have never paddled a canoe or kayak before, don't attempt to jump in a boat and take off on the most grueling trip in this guide, even if you consider yourself to be in good physical shape. Paddling a canoe or kayak exercises different muscles than what you might be accustomed to using. Strong winds and/or tides can exhaust even veteran paddlers.

Furthermore, even if you have paddled before, navigating the torturous maze of islands and channels can be mentally taxing. Start with trips that are easy to navigate and then as you grow more comfortable paddling among the islands and using your chart and compass, work up to the more demanding routes. Try using a local guide to help you learn the area.

Hazards

When people think of the hazards associated with paddling in the Big Cypress Swamp and 10,000 Islands, as in other parts of the Everglades, they typically think first of alligators. Alligators pose little threat to paddlers. The only really dangerous alligators are those that are fed by people, so never feed an alligator. Not only is feeding any wildlife (this includes everything from crows to dolphins) on state and federal lands in Florida illegal and punishable by fine, but feeding eventually spells the end for an alligator because it is soon deemed a *nuisance* and destroyed. Also, someone else may get hurt. Remember, a fed gator is a dead gator. Feeding any wild animal alters its behavior and can make it less capable of surviving in the wild.

Crocodiles live in the 10,000 Islands as well, but they are very shy and if you see one you should consider yourself extremely fortunate. Consider yourself fortunate to see snakes as well.

Biting insects are more a nuisance than a hazard. If you are allergic to stings or bites from anything, remember to pack the appropriate medicine to counteract allergic reactions.

Probably the biggest hazards you'll face paddling are storms, high winds, and strong tides. Bays can get extremely rough and capsize or sink a boat if you are not careful. Heed storm warnings, choose alternate routes to paddle if high winds are forecasted, and remember to check tides to avoid getting stranded or having to paddle against strong current. An ample supply of common sense is one of the best survival tools you can pack.

Heat-Related Illnesses

Remember to take appropriate precautions against heat-related illnesses while on the water. Big Cypress Swamp and the 10,000 Islands are in the subtropics and it can get hot and humid even in January and February. Paddling is a strenuous activity. The combination can result in dehydration, heat exhaustion, and even heat stroke. You should bring at least one gallon of water per person for every day you paddle. Sports drinks will work as well and replace lost electrolytes, but don't rely on sodas or caffeine drinks to keep you sufficiently hydrated. Needless to say, save the beer until after your trip.

Drink water even when you're not thirsty. Snacks such as nuts or crackers will help replace salts you lose when you sweat. If your urine is dark yellow, you're probably not drinking enough. Symptoms of dehydration may include thirst, light-headedness, confusion, and less-frequent urination. Start drinking more water if you experience any of these symptoms and get off the water if you need to. Ignoring these symptoms can lead to heat exhaustion.

Symptoms of heat exhaustion include cool, clammy skin; excessive sweating; fatigue and weakness; dizziness; headache; nausea; muscle cramps; and possibly a weak, rapid pulse. Try to get to shade, drink water, and eat a salty snack. Cool yourself by placing ice from a cooler in a bandana and wrapping it around your neck against your skin. Heat exhaustion ends your trip and you should return to your launch site as soon as you or your companion is capable.

Heat stroke is a serious medical emergency and unlike heat exhaustion can strike suddenly. Heat stroke is caused when you become dehydrated and can't sweat enough to cool off. Your body's cooling system fails and you rapidly overheat. This can be brought on by vigorous activity in high heat and humidity. Symptoms may include headache, dizziness, disorientation or agitation, sluggishness, possible seizure, hallucinations, flushed dry skin that is not sweating, high body temperature, loss of consciousness, and rapid heart rate. Your heart and breathing may stop. If you are paddling alone, don't let yourself get in this situation. Call for emergency help and soak your clothes with water or ice to lower your body temperature. If heat stroke affects your paddling companion, again call for emergency care and attempt to lower their temperature by soaking their clothing with water or ice. Find shade. You may have to perform CPR if the person stops breathing and has no pulse.

Lightning Safety

Florida is the lightning capitol of the world and thunderstorms can occur any time of year. Any thunderhead (cumulonimbus cloud) can produce lightning, even if it's not raining. Lightning can strike as far as 10 miles away from any rainfall and can occur even with blue sky over your head. If you hear thunder, you need to get off the water. Keep the following guidelines in mind any time you paddle:

Get a weather forecast before you leave. Consider bringing a NOAA weather radio to alert you of approaching bad weather. If possible storms are predicted, choose a route that allows you to quickly retreat to shore if a storm threatens.

Watch for dark clouds and increasing wind. Be wary of thunderheads with very dark bases, even if there is no wind, thunder, or lightning. Paddle to a point where you can get off the water within a few minutes.

If you hear thunder or see lightning, get off the water immediately. The sound of thunder travels about 1 mile in 5 seconds. To estimate the distance to a lightning strike, count the number of seconds it takes to hear the thunder after you see the lightning flash. For example, if you hear thunder 15 seconds after you saw the flash, lightning struck about 3 miles away.

If you get caught in a thunderstorm in open water, stay as low as you possibly can in your boat. Lightning typically strikes the highest object, and on the water, that is you. If you can reach land, beach your craft (or lash it to a mangrove if in the swamp) and find a place away from tall trees to crouch as low as you can with your feet close together. Keep your hands off the ground and stay out of the water. A large grove of small mangroves may be a suitable sanctuary.

If you can make it back to a marina or to where you launched, re-treat to a sturdy building and stay away from windows and doors. If no building is available, get to your car (as long as it's a metal hardtop) and roll up your windows.

Wear your PFD. Lightning strike victims often survive, but not if you fall into the water unconscious and sink.

Know CPR. Lightning strike victims are often only stunned and can be revived with CPR.

Tides

The tidal range in the 10,000 Islands is less than 5 feet, but a tremen-dous volume of water drawing from a vast area moves with the tides, so the flow in and out of the passes can be quite strong. I indicate at the beginning of many routes at what tide to paddle. For some of the routes, in particular those requiring a shuttle, you may be able to re-verse the route described in the book to take advantage of a more fa-vorable tide. In general, for trips from Everglades City and Chokoloskee that journey to offshore islands, leave on an outgoing tide and return on an incoming tide. It is no fun paddling against the tide coming through the passes. Make sure to allow for the difference in tide times from the mouth of a pass and locations inland, such as Everglades City or the mouth of the Lopez River.

Wind also has a strong impact on tides here. A strong south or southwest wind may push additional water through the passes, causing higher than normal tides. Conversely, a strong east wind may keep a lot of water from coming in with the tide, creating lower than normal tides. A strong wind blowing across a tide moving in the opposite direction will cause rough and potentially dangerous water. Try to avoid this situation.

The Everglades National Park Gulf Coast Ranger Station and virtually every marina or tackle store in the 10,000 Islands offer a free tide chart. You can also plan ahead and print out your own by accessing tide predictions on the Internet at the following address: www.co-ops.nos. noaa.gov

How to Use the Guide

I have tried to create an assortment of routes in this guide that are interesting to everyone and suitable for a variety of skill levels from beginners to advanced Everglades paddlers. The book is organized into chapters by launch site progressing from west to east from Marco Island to Chokoloskee. Each route begins with a brief description of the route and trip highlights that indicate required charts, trip rating, estimated paddling time and distance, hazards, launch site, route ownership and phone number, and an alternate route if one exists or is warranted. An expanded description of the route follows, detailing various legs of the route, approximate distance, landmarks, and what you might expect to see.

I suggest you go over each route using the written description and the map in the guide with your compass and nautical chart before you actually paddle it. You can then make any notes on your nautical chart with a waterproof pen. If you don't want to mark up your chart, make a photocopy of the area you want to paddle and mark that up. Stow it in a waterproof bag with your charts for reference if you need it.

Make certain you tell someone where you are going before you leave, such as a relative or friend at home or the front desk clerk of your motel. That way if you don't return when expected, someone will know to call and send authorities to look for you. Cell phone coverage is unreliable and you can't always count on a cell phone in an emergency. If you change your plans, make sure you relay the change in plans.

Distances

The convoluted nature of the waterways in this region enabled me to supply estimated distances only. Use the map provided with each route to help follow the narration, but do not rely on it for navigation or as a substitute for a compass and the appropriate chart. Arrows point in the direction of travel I describe on the route, but remember you may be able to reverse the direction of a trip if conditions dictate.

Mileage over land by vehicle to launch sites is stated in statute miles, while paddling distances are given in nautical miles to correspond with the nautical charts required to navigate the routes. If you are using a GPS, make certain you set your units of measurement to nautical miles when you are on the water. Your speed will then be measured in knots: 1 knot corresponds to 1 nautical mile per hour, and 1 nautical mile is approximately 1.15 statute miles.

Natural History

For most of the last several million years, southern Florida has been covered by a warm, shallow sea. Countless marine creatures lived and died and added their remains to layer upon layer of marine sediment. The Big Cypress Swamp and 10,000 Islands we know today have been around for fewer than 6,000 years, built upon limestone bedrock comprised of those marine sediments and populated by a unique blend of plants and animals of tropical and temperate origins. Although the terrain appears tediously flat, the landscape you see occupies a natural series of peaks and valleys ranging in height from a few inches below sea level to a whopping 5 feet above sea level. The whole region slopes downward at about 2 inches per mile, causing a wide sheet of rain water to flow slowly over 2,400 square miles of southwest Florida from just south of Lake Okeechobee to the Gulf of Mexico. This water channels in the larger sloughs (pronounced slews) of Big Cypress Swamp, including Okaloacoochee Slough, Fakahatchee Strand, New River Strand, Gator Hook Strand, and Sweetwater Strand, which in turn may spawn rivers that wriggle through mangrove swamps into the estuaries of the 10,000 Islands.

Big Cypress Swamp is named not so much for the size of its trees, though historically giant cypress trees were common here, but rather for the extent of area covered by cypress. Most of the cypress are found in strands (long, narrow strips of swamp following valleys in the limestone), domes (which look like hills, with tall trees in the center and smaller ones at the edges), and prairies. The biggest trees are found in the strands, where they have an ample supply of peat soil, water, and nutrients; while the smallest trees, the dwarf cypress, spread across wide prairies with their roots anchored in little more than a film of soil and limestone bedrock.

But the Big Cypress Swamp is more than cypress. Even within the sloughs and strands, red maple, oaks, willows, pop ash, pond apples, and even royal palms join with cypress to create a mixed hardwood swamp. Slash pine forests and stands of palmettos find footholds on ridges of limestone rising above wide prairies of mixed grasses. Toward the southern end of Big Cypress Swamp, the freshwater landscape melds into one that is estuarine, a brackish mix of sweetwater sheet flow and salt water from the Gulf of Mexico. Mangrove forest dominates the coast of this estuarine landscape, the largest in North America. Coastal prairies of salt-tolerant grasses and tropical hardwood hammocks perched on the shell mound remnants of the ancient Calusa civilization punctuate the mangroves. Extending seaward beyond the coastal forest are shallow brackish bays, mangrove islands, oyster bars, tidal mudflats, sea grass beds, and finally the open waters of the Gulf of Mexico. Sea level is on the rise again and the rising ocean water is what many scientists think give the offshore mangrove islands their irregular, puzzlelike shapes.

Most people visiting the Everglades and Big Cypress Swamp expect to see wildlife, and they are rarely disappointed. Although the variety and numbers of wildlife are diminished from what existed prior to the arrival of European settlers, the tapestry is still rich. More than 300

Wading Birds

Wading birds, primarily members of the taxonomic order *Ciconiiformes,* comprise a loose grouping of wetland-dependent, long-legged birds that include herons, egrets, bitterns, ibises, spoonbills, and storks. Wood storks are the only North American storks and are more closely related taxonomically to New World (North and South American) vultures than they are to other wading birds.

Most wading birds are colonial nesters who defend small territories within the colony. These nesting colonies are called rookeries. Wading birds often feed and sleep in groups even outside of the nesting season. They typically raise a single brood a year, laying three to five eggs in a platformlike stick nest from the previous year, or one that has been scavenged close to the old one. Eggs incubate for two to five weeks, and the chicks fledge in four to eight weeks, depending on species. Some wading birds may live for more than 20 years in the wild.

Limpkins and cranes are wading birds from the order *Gruiformes,* which also includes rails and gallinules, and they share few traits with other wading birds except their dependence on wetlands for survival. The sandhill crane and whooping crane are the two native crane species in North America.

Herons and egrets specialize in taking fish and other aquatic creatures, but they aren't picky and can take anything from backyard squirrels to the chicks and eggs of shorebirds. If they can get it down their skinny throat,

Tricolored heron

they will eat it. Some wading birds stalk, some (such as the reddish egret) have quite vigorous hunting techniques, and some employ both (snowy egrets and tricolored herons fly and snap or patiently stalk.) Researchers have observed more than 30 different feeding behaviors among the herons and egrets alone. The black-crowned night heron and green heron are reported to even fish with bait, including insects, twigs, seeds, bread, and flowers. Some wading birds, such as the wood stork and roseate spoonbill, have extremely sensitive beaks and forage by touch. Most wading birds forage during the daytime, but some such as the bittern and night herons feed at night. Great blue herons often fish on moonlit nights. The white ibis and less common glossy ibis are the most highly gregarious Florida wading birds in both feeding and roosting.

Many adult herons and egrets have more than one color form called plumage polymorphism by ornithologists. For example, the reddish egret comes in a reddish and a white form; the great blue heron comes in a white form (great white heron), mixed form of white and blue (Wierdeman's heron), and the more common and widespread blue form. The great white heron and Wierdeman's heron are restricted to south Florida. This is in addition to the immature white coloration of many herons that confound casual birders because they very closely resemble egrets. For example, the little blue heron is white for its first year and is easily confused with snowy egrets, cattle egrets, and white-form reddish egrets.

During the breeding season, herons and egrets develop elaborate nuptial plumes on the head, neck, and back called aigrettes. They show off these plumes prominently during spectacular courtship displays prior to mating. The legs and bills may also change color during courtship, which can really confuse identification for a novice. Most wading birds that breed in colonies are seasonally monogamous.

Herons and egrets were nearly shot to extinction in the late 19th and early 20th centuries for their breeding plumes. This was doubly disturbing because not only were thousands of adult birds killed during breeding season, but young birds were often left to starve on the nest, eliminating the next generation. The slaughter and subsequent fight to save these birds from extinction was a critical struggle that laid the groundwork for today's conservation movement. The destruction or degradation of habitat remains the greatest threat to wading birds today. The use of DDT and similar pesticides still affect species such as spoonbills in their southern wintering grounds in countries where the use of these pesticides has not been banned.

Cranes are large, long-legged birds that may stand as tall as 4 feet. They have stouter bodies and a shorter neck and beak than herons. Cranes are generally omnivorous, picking food off the ground or digging it up with their beak. Unlike other wading birds, they do not nest in colonies and do not build a stick nest. Instead they choose a new nest site each year, building a platform from surrounding reeds and grasses and encircling it with a moat. Cranes mate for life and perform enchanting dancing displays for one another. Cranes produce one brood per year, typically laying two eggs that hatch asynchronously after four or five weeks. Young cranes may take as long as 18 weeks to fledge, although they are able run around and forage very soon after hatching. The sandhill crane is probably the only crane you'll see in the 10,000 Islands. The whooping crane has been reintroduced to Florida, but its range does not currently extend into the Everglades.

species of birds are resident or pass through during seasonal migrations. The dry season is the best time to see birds because many are wintering and others congregate around pooling water sources to take advantage of fish, frogs, and other food concentrated in the dwindling water. In a single small pond, you may see a variety of ducks, every species of wading bird found in Florida, white pelicans, black-necked stilts, moorhens, grebes, and for good measure, a bald eagle and an osprey eyeing one another from the tops of dead cabbage palms. An astounding number of small songbirds trills and chortles from the canopies of pine and cypress forests.

Mammals include Florida black bear, Florida panther, bobcat, white-tailed deer, river otter, Everglades mink, and various mice and rats, in addition to raccoons, bottle-nosed dolphins, and West Indian manatees. These are the animals paddlers are most likely to see on the water. Alligators are common and lucky paddlers might see a shy American crocodile or mangrove terrapin. More than 40 species of fish live in fresh and estuarine waters, including striped mullet (which may jump in your boat), spotted sea trout, snook, and tarpon.

The whole cycle of life in Big Cypress Swamp and 10,000 Islands is driven by rainfall and a well-defined wet season and dry season. Unlike the eastern Everglades, the Big Cypress Swamp watershed is fed only by rainfall. It is not directly connected to Lake Okeechobee or any river. Like the eastern Everglades it receives an average of 55–60 inches of rain a year, most of which falls during tumultuous afternoon thunderstorms

A brown spiny seastar

from June through November, the rainy season. Water levels in the swamp begin to drop in November as afternoon thunderstorms diminish, marking the onset of the dry season; and by the beginning of June, fresh water is often confined to deep sloughs and alligator holes. Periodic hurricanes flatten mangrove forests, redirect passes, and reshape or even virtually eliminate islands, setting the stage for new life to rise from the devastation.

Human History

Humans have been living in the Big Cypress Swamp and 10,000 Islands for thousands of years. The first Native American inhabitants were probably ancestors to the Calusa. The Calusa were a nonagricultural people with a rich and diverse culture. Archeological evidence and written accounts by Spanish explorers suggest they ate shellfish (including clams and oysters and crabs), deer, small mammals, possibly manatees, fish, alligators and other reptiles, and birds. They did not have flint for tools, and trading with other Native American groups was limited, so they relied instead on hard materials such as shells, wood, bones, shark teeth, and vegetable fibers. For example, conch shells were fitted with wooden handles for digging, cutting, and pounding tools. They made knives by setting shark teeth into wooden handles.

Shell mounds, the most obvious evidence of Calusa civilization that remains, are found throughout the western Everglades from Marco Island south to Shark Island, including Sandfly Island and Russell Key. A complex of 30 undisturbed mounds is situated near the mouth of Turner River. Other large mounds occurred on Chokoloskee and Marco Islands, but these have been extensively degraded by removal of fill and leveling. The Calusa built some shell mounds as refuse heaps, while others may have been intended for interment. All shell mounds provided useful high ground in case of storm surges during hurricanes. About 2,000 Calusa are estimated to have lived in southwest Florida at the time of their first contact with the Spanish in some 30 villages that may have included as many as 200 people. Because of the warm climate, men wore little more than a palm breech cloth, and women may have worn only a Spanish moss skirt around the waist. Spanish accounts describe them as ornately tattooed and painted. Bows and arrows were the principal weapons, but they also used clubs and spears. Spears were thrown with an atlatl, or spear thrower.

The Calusa were gone by 1800, primarily victims of European diseases for which they had no defense. The last of the Calusa may have sailed with the Spanish to Cuba when Florida was surrendered to the British in 1763.

Native Americans had not abandoned Florida however. Because of increasing pressure from white settlers spreading out from the infant United States, survivors from several native Florida tribes mingled in northern Florida with members of other tribal groups forced from their ancestral homes in southeastern North America. The array of groups with diverse languages and customs was referred to by English-speakers as Seminoles, from the Maskókî phrase *istî siminolî* and the Mikisúkî phrase *yat'siminoli,* both meaning free people, because they had never been conquered by Europeans. Seminoles began filtering into southwest Florida as early as the latter 1700s and remain to this day in south Florida despite three different Seminole wars during the 1800s in which the U.S. Army sought to drive them out. The Seminoles have now divided into the Seminole Tribe of Florida and the Miccosukee Tribe of Indians of Florida. The Miccosukees live primarily on a reservation and in scattered villages along the Tamiami Trail between Miami and Naples. The Seminoles live primarily on five different reservations between Tampa and Hollywood.

White settlers began arriving in the mid-1800s and took up residence throughout the 10,000 Islands, particularly on islands with shell mounds. Most of the islands that had enough high ground for a house were settled at one time or another. Thriving little communities developed on Chokoloskee, Sandfly Island, Fakahatchee Island, and at Everglades City, then known as Everglade. Settlers in the 10,000 Islands in the late 1800s and early 1900s fished, farmed, and turtled, and some operated boat services from the islands to Key West. Among the crops grown in the 10,000 Islands were tomatoes and sugar cane. Sugar cane was an important cash crop, particularly when boiled down into syrup. Virtually all traffic was by boat, and settlers looked to Key West for commerce and news. The passes and rivers among islands were the primary travel routes until the 1920s, when Barron Collier arrived with new roads, a railroad, and enterprise. In 1928 the Tamiami Trail was completed and Everglades City was linked by car to the rest of Florida. Virtually all of the Big Cypress Swamp was logged in the 1940s and early 1950s. In 1947 Everglades National Park was established and pioneer life in the 10,000 Islands disappeared forever. Big Cypress National Preserve was established in 1974, primarily in response to a giant jetport that threatened the Everglades watershed.

The livelihoods of people living in Everglades City, Chokoloskee, and communities on Marco Island are now largely dependent on tourism and development that caters to winter residents. Well over a million acres of land and watery wilderness is protected within Big Cypress Swamp and the 10,000 Islands, ready to be explored by canoe and kayak. Let the journey begin.

PART I

Marco Island

The 6,800-acre Marco Island is the largest of the 10,000 Islands. It is surprisingly diverse and includes high sandhills, slash pine forests, and sandy fields, in addition to quartz sand beaches and mangrove swamp. It is the only place in the 10,000 Islands to see burrowing owls. Unfortunately, very little land on the island, if any, is being protected due to aggressive development.

Originally there were three separate towns on Marco Island: Marco, site of the first settlement and now the city of Marco Island; Goodland, at the edge of Goodland Bay at the east side of the island; and Caxambas, on the south side of the island overlooking Caxambas Pass. Caxambas is now a place in name only.

Marco Island was first homesteaded by W. T. Collier and his family in 1870, and he is acknowledged as the founder of Marco. Within several years Marco became a thriving little fishing community and known for clamming, boatbuilding, and sportfishing. Two clam canneries operated at Caxambas and Marco. Clams were originally gathered by hand and later by dredge. The clamming industry survived on the island until 1947. Farming was also important, in particular fruit-growing. Hundreds of acres of sandhills around Caxambas were devoted to pineapple cultivation, and there was even a pineapple packing plant. Apparently folks had a pineapple patch in virtually every backyard along the southwest coast. Citrus was also important.

Barron G. Collier purchased 90 percent of Marco Island in 1922,

Osprey

Paddlers in the 10,000 Islands often are delighted by the sight of an osprey dropping in front of them from 200 feet to grasp a wriggling fish in its talons. You may notice bulky nests on channel markers ringing with the whistles and chirps of a parent osprey and hungry chicks. Ospreys are common throughout Florida and live here year-round. Outside Florida ospreys are typically less common and are generally migratory. Ospreys feed almost entirely on fish that they catch by dropping into the water with feet outstretched. Their feet have spines, in addition to talons, to allow them to better grip slippery, wriggling prey. The feathers are dense and oily to allow the birds to shed water, and the short stiff feathers of their long legs allow the bird to crash through the water with minimum resistance. After catching a fish, an osprey often rests with its catch at the surface for a moment before lifting off. Occasionally an osprey grabs a fish too large for it to lift from the water, and unable to unlock its talons, may drown. Large fish have been caught with osprey skeletons attached to their backs. Sometimes an osprey is able to flounder ashore with its oversized catch and eat it there, or tear enough off that it can fly with the remains.

Ospreys are dark brown and white, with a white head and white underparts and a dark brown eye stripe. As with most raptors, ospreys are sexually dimorphic, meaning males and females look somewhat different. Females are generally larger, and the pattern of chocolate and white varies slightly from the male. Females often have a brown speckled band across the chest. An osprey's wingspan may reach more than 5 feet, and the wings are bent at the elbows, like a gull, when in flight. The white underparts and bent wings are what best helps identify ospreys from bald eagles in flight.

excluding the remainder of the island owned by the other Collier family. In 1949 the entire community of Caxambas literally picked up and moved across the island to Goodland, houses and all. Goodland was considered better suited as a fishing village, and the Collier Company had development plans for Caxambas. Collier Company paid for the move on the condition that the residents, most of them squatters, bought their lots at Goodland. Goodland still remains a relatively laid-back fishing village, in contrast to high-rent Marco Island.

As late as the mid-1960s, Marco Island was a sleepy little island, and most folks thought any real development would occur on Cape Ro-

Visitors to the 10,000 Islands see ospreys nesting on navigational markers, large exposed mangroves, large cypress, and even power poles along roadsides. The nests are huge, brushy affairs that the birds use year after year. Ospreys do not form life partners, but they are generally monogamous during the nesting season and return to the same mate each year. Polygyny, where a male will mate with more than one female in a season, seems to occur only when there is high male mortality. The female lays three eggs and does most of the incubating. The male is responsible for feeding her during incubation. After four to six weeks, the eggs hatch, and the male continues to hunt and the female feeds and broods the chicks. Both the eggs and chicks are camouflaged to help protect them against the predators. The female rarely leaves the nest as an additional measure of protection. Osprey chicks fledge a couple of months after hatching and become sexually mature after three to five years. Ospreys may live to 13 years or so.

Ospreys seem common enough in the 10,000 Islands, but during the 1960s and 1970s, their numbers declined dramatically due to eggshell thinning caused by DDT and other related pesticides. Thin eggshells caused the eggs to crack before the chicks were ready to hatch, and reproductive success plummeted. Although ospreys are found on every continent except Antarctica, they are quite rare in some countries due to the residual effects of pesticide use and past pressure by egg collectors. Visitors from Britain or Scotland, for example, are amazed to see more ospreys in one outing in the 10,000 Islands than exist in all of the United Kingdom. Habitat loss, primarily lack of trees or structures suitable for nesting, continues to plague ospreys, although they do seem ready to utilize almost any suitable platform from idle construction cranes to man-made nest platforms.

mano, not Marco. Now Cape Romano and Kice Island are protected within the Rookery Bay National Estuarine Research Reserve, and Marco Island is almost completely developed, replete with high-rise beachfront condominiums. The modern concrete bridges linking Marco Island and the neighboring Isles of Capri with the mainland doomed the island to development.

Marco Island is perhaps best known for the artifacts recovered from Calusa shell mounds. The Marco Island dig, excavated in 1896 by the Pepper-Hurst Archeological Expedition led by Frank Hamilton Cushing, yielded the largest quantity of Calusa artifacts ever discovered.

The find, preserved by peat and anaerobic mud, included rare wooden ornaments, some with paint remaining. There were also ceremonial masks, bowls, dugout canoes, a carved deer head, and weapons. Shell mounds on Marco Island were later augmented by cast-off shells from the island's two clam canneries, the last of which closed in 1947. Nearly all of the shell mounds now have buildings perched upon them. The shell mounds on Goodland, unfortunately, have been extensively dredged and leveled.

The main attraction for paddlers is Rookery Bay National Estuarine Research Reserve, which encompasses Rookery Bay, its namesake, and 110,000 acres of uplands, islands, and estuaries from Gordon Pass at Naples to Everglades National Park. Some 150 species of birds live in the estuarine research reserve, including bald eagles, ospreys, roseate spoonbills, black skimmers, and least terns. Management of Rookery Bay is a cooperative effort between Florida Department of Environmental Protection's Office of Coastal and Aquatic Managed Areas and the National Oceanic and Atmospheric Administration (NOAA). Rookery Bay is one of three such estuarine research reserves in Florida and part of the National Estuarine Research Reserve System. Rookery Bay emphasizes land management, restoration, research, and education.

Rookery Bay is opening a new 16,500-square-foot visitors center and marine laboratory in late 2003. To reach the visitors center and headquarters, located between Marco and Naples, turn right off CR 951 south of US 41 on Tower Road. You can also access a canoe trail through Rookery Bay and visit The Conservancy's Briggs Nature Center by turning right off CR 951 on Shell Island Road, just south of the Rookery Bay headquarters.

The paddling routes covered in this section offer one trip that launches from the Caxambas Park boat ramp on the west side of Marco Island and two trips that launch from the Goodland Bridge at the east side of the island.

1. Kice Island and Cape Romano

Trip highlights: Beautiful beaches, sheltered backwater paddling, good birding, dolphins and manatees in the passes

Charts/maps: NOAA Nautical Chart #11430, the waterproof Pasadena Top Spot Fishing Map N-204

Trip rating: Easy to Moderate

Estimated total time: 7–8 hours

Total distance: About 14 nautical miles round trip

Hazards: Powerboats, jet skis, strong wind and tide, shallows in Morgan Bay

Launch site: Caxambas Park boat ramp (no fee for canoes or kayaks if you don't pull a trailer)

Ownership: Rookery Bay National Estuarine Research Reserve (239-417-6310)

Alternate routes: If the Gulf is calm, paddle the west side along the beach to Morgan Point on Cape Romano. Shorten this route by cutting through Blind Pass to circle Kice Island only.

General Information

This is a scenic loop route to Kice Island and Cape Romano, two undeveloped barrier islands south of Marco Island. Cape Romano was reputed in the 1800s as the only place in the area with a good supply of fresh water, a reason for the early settlement there. Spanish explorer Juan Ponce de León called the place "Manataca" and stopped there with troops in 1513, apparently winding up in a pitched daylong battle with the Calusa, who had heard about his cruelty toward natives. During the Third Seminole War, Cape Romano served briefly as a camp for U.S. forces warring with Spanish Indians in the Florida Keys.

The islands are included within the Rookery Bay National Estuarine Research Reserve and are left to nature now. This route takes you from the boat ramp at Caxambas Park along the western shore of Kice Island to Snook Hole Key, then across to explore a creek in Helen Key, before scooting back across Snook Hole Pass to the Morgan River and on to Morgan Beach on Cape Romano.

Morgan Beach and Kice Island offer idyllic sandy beaches where

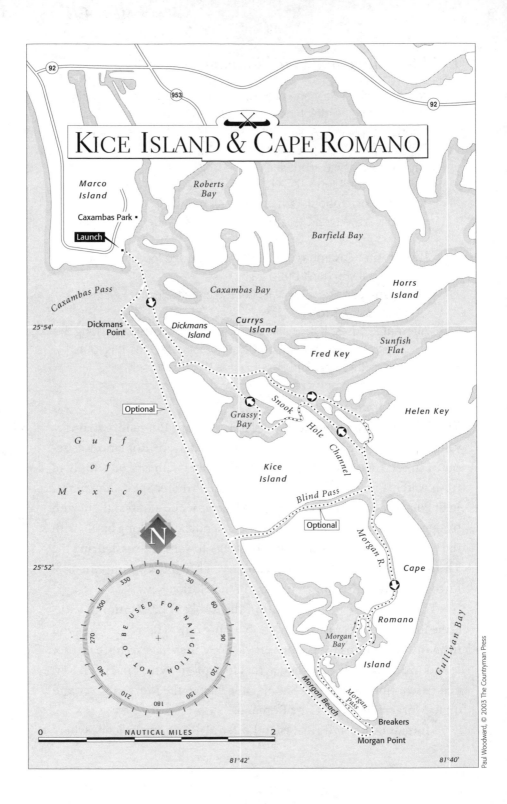

KICE ISLAND & CAPE ROMANO

Marco Island

Caxambas Park

Launch

Roberts Bay

Barfield Bay

Caxambas Pass

Dickmans Point

Dickmans Island

Caxambas Bay

Currys Island

Horrs Island

Fred Key

Sunfish Flat

Optional

Grassy Bay

Snook

Hole

Channel

Helen Key

G u l f

o f

M e x i c o

Kice Island

Blind Pass

Optional

Morgan R.

Cape

N

NOT TO BE USED FOR NAVIGATION

Romano

Morgan Bay

Island

Gullivan Bay

Morgan Pass

Morgan Beach

Breakers

Morgan Point

0   NAUTICAL MILES   2

25°54'

25°52'

81°42'

81°40'

loggerhead sea turtles come to lay their eggs during the summer. Look for manatees and dolphins in the passes and wading birds among the mangroves in narrow creeks and the Morgan River. Stingrays are quite common in this area, and you may see them skittering across the surface of a bay. Do the *stingray shuffle* if you venture off the beach into the water. There are three privately owned abandoned houses on Morgan Beach that are falling into the Gulf of Mexico. Try to avoid paddling Morgan Bay during low tide.

Access
From I-75 take Exit 101 (last exit before toll) to CR 951 (Collier Boulevard). Travel CR 951 south 7 miles to Marco Island. Once you cross the bridge to Marco Island, continue on CR 951 (Collier Boulevard) 4½ miles to Caxambas Park, which is on your right near the end of the road. Double-check that there is no ramp fee for canoes and kayaks. The boat ramp office does not have a listed phone number. There is no overnight parking.

Route
Head south/southeast from the Caxambas Park boat ramp to paddle between Dickmans Point and Dickmans Island. If the Gulf of Mexico is calm, consider paddling the Gulf side of Kice Island and Cape Romano, and then follow this route back to the boat ramp. The wind often picks up in the afternoon, so morning is usually the best time to paddle in the Gulf. You'll pass a channel marker with an osprey nest. You will see exotic Australian pines on your right on Dickmans Point, a sign of previous human activity. Pass Dickmans Island on your left; and then about 1 mile from the boat ramp, look toward your right for a cove with a sand landing. You may see other boats there. There is a little path leading to the Gulf beach and an interesting shoreline littered with dead trees. Walk north a few hundred feet to a little beach on which to sun. Walk south to explore the shoreline of shattered trees.

Continue on your trip by paddling out of the cove and heading east following the channel markers to Snook Hole Channel at about a 100-degree course. The southeast tip of Dickmans Island, Currys Island, and

View of Cape Romano backwater from Morgan Beach

Fred Key will be on your left. Make sure you stay south of east and follow the channel markers or you'll wind up paddling over Sunfish Flat on the north side of Helen Key, ogling multi-million-dollar homes on Horrs Island to your left and wondering how you got there.

Once you reach Snook Hole Channel, you can cut across to Little Grassy Bay on the inside of Helen Key and paddle through an interesting little creek that may be full of wading birds in the mangroves, including snowy egrets, tricolored herons, white ibis, and maybe even roseate spoonbills. This creek has no name and appears only on the NOAA chart. The creek drops you back out into Snook Hole Channel. Snook Hole Channel may be full of boats and jet skis even on a weekday, so watch out for them.

From the mouth of the creek, paddle due south about ½ mile to the mouth of the Morgan River. If you need to land again and stretch your legs, you'll see a small sandy area on Cape Romano Island in front of you, just left of the mouth of Morgan River. This area may be a little confusing because it is where Morgan River, Blind Pass, and Snook Hole Channel converge. Blind Pass heads off to the west. Morgan River continues south. Snook Hole Channel empties into Gullivan Bay to the east, bounded by Coon Key and Turtle Key in the distance.

After about ¾ mile of paddling on the Morgan River, an island bisects the river and you can paddle either direction around it to continue on the main channel. If you take the path to the right, you will pass two narrow cuts, both of which lead you back to the Morgan River. These won't appear on the chart. Paddling through these narrow creeks on a high incoming tide is like running a river through treetops. You may have to pull yourself through in a couple places.

The Morgan River empties into Morgan Bay, which at low tide is a nightmare to cross. The bay is muddy and gives you little visual indication of its depth. There are PVC markers across the bay indicating a rudimentary channel, but from a kayak you are so close to the water surface that even by following the markers it's hard to stay in the channel. You can make it across, but ideally avoid the bay at low tide.

If you have enough water to paddle directly across Morgan Bay, head southwest to loop just inside Carr Island and enter Morgan Pass. There are plenty of places to land on Morgan Beach to your right or on Cape Romano to your left. Morgan Beach offers bright white sand, sea oats, and good shelling. Watch for breakers at the mouth of Morgan Pass near Morgan Point. You may also see the three abandoned houses falling into the sea, victims of the barrier island's slow eastward migration.

When you're ready to return to Marco Island, you can paddle around Morgan Point into the Gulf of Mexico, if conditions are calm enough, or return across Morgan Bay through the Morgan River out to Snook Hole Channel and Blind Pass. From this point you can paddle west through Blind Pass to reach the Gulf of Mexico, then paddle the western shore of Kice Island. If there is a strong westerly wind, stay on the inside route following Snook Hole Channel north and then northeast, keeping Kice Island close on your left. After paddling just under 1 mile, you will see a mangrove creek cutting away on your left. Follow this creek as it courses a wandering west toward Grassy Bay. As you paddle out of Grassy Bay, keep the shoreline of Kice Island to your left and follow the channel markers northwest past Dickmans Island on your right. Watch for manatees at the edge of the channel. From Dickmans Point adjust your course north to paddle across Caxambas Pass and return to the boat ramp. Use the eight-story, blue-and-gray building as a landmark.

2.   *Shell Key Loop*

Trip highlights: Beautiful beaches, sheltered mangrove creeks, open bays, good birding, dolphins in the passes

Charts/maps: NOAA Nautical Chart #11430, Waterproof Chart #40E

Trip rating: Easy to Moderate

Estimated total time: 6–7 hours

Total distance: About 14 nautical miles round trip

Hazards: Powerboats, airboats, strong wind and tide, shallows in Palm Bay and upper creeks

Launch site: Goodland Bridge

Ownership: Rookery Bay National Estuarine Research Reserve (239-417-6310)

Alternate routes: Shorten route by about 3 miles by paddling south out of Blackwater Bay using Southwest Gate Pass and Whitney Channel to reach Gullivan Bay.

General Information

The loop route around Shell Key and the islands of Gullivan Bay is a long, meandering paddle that begins along the northern edge of Goodland Bay and passes into Palm Bay through quiet creeks and shallow small bays. The mudflats and oyster bars are lovely, and you can ride the incoming tide, so the paddling is easy. You navigate around the southern end of Palm Bay and then pass into oyster-riddled Blackwater Bay, south of Collier-Seminole State Park, perhaps pausing to cast a few times to big sea trout or redfish off the bars. The route then takes you from Blackwater Bay into Buttonwood Bay and around the east and

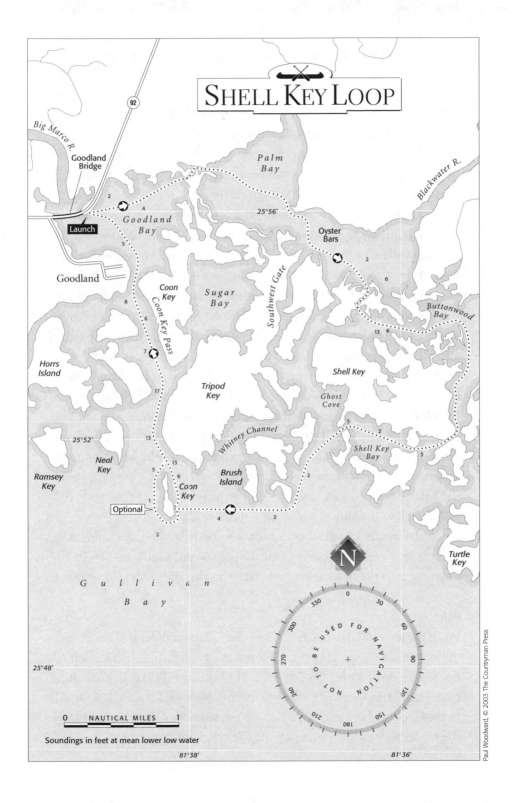

SHELL KEY LOOP

Big Marco R.

92

Goodland Bridge

Palm Bay

25°56'

Blackwater R.

2

4

Goodland Bay

Launch

Oyster Bars

5

2

Goodland

Coon Key

Sugar Bay

Southwest Gate

6

8

Coon Key Pass

6

7

Buttonwood Bay

13 6

Horrs Island

17

Shell Key

Ghost Cove

Tripod Key

5

25°52'

13

Whitney Channel

Shell Key Bay

2

5

Neal Key

13

Ramsey Key

5 6

Brush Island

2

Coon Key

Optional

1

4

2

2

Turtle Key

G u l l i v a n
B a y

N

NOT TO BE USED FOR NAVIGATION

0
30
60
90
120
150
081
210
240
270
300
330

25°48'

0   NAUTICAL MILES   1

Soundings in feet at mean lower low water

81°38'

81°36'

Paul Woodward, © 2003 The Countryman Press

south sides of Shell Key into Shell Key Bay. From Shell Key Bay onward, the route covers open water, traversing northern Gullivan Bay past several wild sandy islands and then following Coon Key Pass back past the village of Goodland and your return to the Goodland Bridge.

You will need the NOAA Nautical Chart #11430 to navigate the part of the route west of Palm Bay and Tripod Key, and you can rely on the Waterproof Chart #40E for Blackwater Bay and Shell Key. You may find it helpful to refer between them during the trip.

It's hard to strongly recommend a best tide for this route because at some point along the way you will encounter current running against you, regardless of the tide on which you launched. However, the tide doesn't seem to rip through these passes quite like those in Everglades National Park. Your best bet is to launch at the middle of an incoming tide to ride through the coastal creeks and navigate Palm and Blackwater Bays. The early stages of an incoming tide offer the best birding and views of the wonderful creatures that patrol oyster bars and mud banks; but if good water is what you care about, wait for the middle of an incoming tide. If you don't rush, you should make Shell Key in time to ride a tide just turning to drain creeks and passes around Shell Key. After you paddle Shell Key Bay and enter the open waters of Gullivan Bay, you can idle the hours of the outgoing tide away by island hopping and exploring beaches, saving Coon Key or Tripod Key for last. When the tide turns again and begins to flow into Coon Key Pass, ride this water back to the launch site at Goodland Bridge.

If the weather forecast calls for the wind to build in the afternoon, reverse this route to travel Coon Key Pass and Gullivan Bay in the morning and the more sheltered waters in the afternoon, tide willing.

Access

From the town of Marco, take CR 953 (San Marco Boulevard) east, which turns into CR 92, cross over the Goodland Bridge, and then launch on the south side of the bridge. From US 41 (Tamiami Trail) and the flashing caution light just west of Collier-Seminole State Park, take CR 92 south to the Goodland Bridge and pull off on the left side of the road just before the bridge to launch. The launch may be muddy at low tide.

Along the Shell Key route

Route

Launch from the Goodland Bridge on the southeast side and paddle east. Pass through the gap between the headlands off your bow and the island to your right. Continue paddling east/northeast into Goodland Bay toward the next headland. Goodland Bay is muddy and shallow at low tide. After passing this next headland, angle northeast and paddle toward the northeast corner of the bay, keeping fairly close to the shoreline on the left. At about ¾ mile from the bridge at the northeast end of the bay, you are faced with a wall of mangroves and the choice to turn left or right. Turn left. Continue paddling north/northeast through a creek, staying north past another opportunity to turn east. This is a beautiful creek and you may pass a variety of shorebirds feeding or resting on the mudflats, including willets, spotted sandpipers, and dowitchers. At just over 1 mile from the bridge, the creek makes a hairpin turn around a mangrove point and bends back to the southeast. Keep to your left shoreline as the creek opens into a small bay and paddle east toward the gap in the mangroves at the east end of the bay.

About 1¾ miles from the bridge, you enter Palm Bay. If you have lots of water, you can paddle southeast at about 140 degrees directly across the bay. Otherwise, follow the mangrove and oyster bar shoreline on your right to navigate the lower bay, still keeping a general southeast heading toward the lower east corner of the bay. At the southeast corner of the bay is a cut that connects to Blackwater Bay (Blackwater Bay is labeled as oyster bars on the NOAA chart). If you were previously riding an incoming tide through the creeks, it now runs against you in this pass as water pours through Blackwater Bay into Palm Bay. Stay to the left shoreline until you reach the junction of what looks like a quieter, broad swath of moving water leading east to an open bay. Paddle a wandering southeast toward open Blackwater Bay.

Paddle across Blackwater Bay approximately 1 mile southeast on a wandering 120 degrees heading to reach the next pass, which drops south toward Shell Key. You pass channel markers leading boaters into Blackwater River halfway across the bay. If you don't have enough water to make it across, pick your way along the southern edge of Blackwater Bay by hugging the right shoreline. You'll first pass one gap that leads to Lighter Bay and a second gap that leads to an unnamed bay. The third gap is a channel that leads straight south to Gullivan Bay, skirting the eastern edge of Southwest Gate and Tripod Key. Follow this to shorten your trip and bypass Shell Key.

Continue paddling southeast across Blackwater Bay to the channel markers. These are about 3¾ miles from your launch point at Goodland Bridge. Here you intersect the Blackwater River Trail. Just past the channel markers, look for trail marker 9 and follow it northeast to trail marker 10. At marker 10 turn right and head southeast about 100 degrees. Look for a pass guarded by oyster bars in the southeast corner of the bay. Paddle a wandering south to reach a wide channel and Shell Key in front of you. Turn left and paddle east to follow the channel into the top of Buttonwood Bay, about 5½ miles from your launch at Goodland Bridge.

From your entrance into the bay, paddle southeast toward the tip of what looks like a necklace of mangrove and oyster islets. At the tip of the necklace, turn southwest at about 210 degrees to drop into a channel at the edge of Shell Key. The shoreline is quite confusing, but there are three passes that all lead to virtually the same point at the southeast corner of Shell Key, so don't sweat it if you find yourself paddling in the wrong channel. You may encounter airboats running one of the passes through here. The tide really flows through these passes, but you can paddle against the current without much problem. All of the passes are very scenic.

If you nailed the right pass, it will run south before turning sharply southwest and back southeast. You'll encounter a mangrove creek wandering away to your right just as the creek widens and you near the larger pass that you will follow to Shell Key Bay. When you reach the confluence of passes at just under 7 miles from Goodland Bridge, you'll be faced with several options. You will turn right and paddle southwest and then west about ½ mile into Shell Key Bay.

Paddle west/northwest across Shell Key Bay. Watch for shoals in the middle of the bay. As you approach the west end of the bay, look for white sand beaches through a cut off your bow, or to your left, depending on how far north in the bay you are paddling. Paddle through the cut and into a very wide unnamed channel that may simply be the eastern fork of Whitney Channel. Tazz Key is directly off your bow and Ghost Cove is to your right. Paddle southwest to land at the sand beach of the unnamed mangrove island south of Tazz Key. There is shade in the mangroves to eat lunch, and the fishing for redfish is good. The beach allows you to look east and see the beaches of Turtle Key and Gullivan Key in the distance. The little cove is nice for a cooling dip, but watch for stingrays. Shuffle if you walk around in the water. You actually have a couple of choices for sandy beaches, including one idyllic little island right in the middle of the channel leading out to Gullivan Bay.

When you're ready to leave this island, paddle around its south tip and into Gullivan Bay. Brush Island will come up on your right as you paddle west. Turn northwest as you pass Brush Island to paddle between Tripod Key and Coon Key. The southwest shores of Brush Island and Tripod Key, as well as much of Coon Key, are fun to explore. There's a wonderful little sand spit on the north tip of Coon Key. Watch for dolphins in the channel between the west shore of Coon Key and Neal Key.

From the air the 10,000 Islands show a significant shape and structure. Geologists describe them as looking like a school of fish swimming in a southeasterly direction—each fish-shaped island having an "eye" of water in its enlarged end, the heads of all the little "fish" pointing to the southeast. —Rachel Carson, *The Edge of the Sea*

Coon Key is about 10 miles from your start at the Goodland Bridge.

From the north tip of Coon Key, paddle northwest through Coon Key Pass back to the Goodland Bridge. Stay off to one side of the channel; or if you have enough water, just paddle outside the channel along the shoreline. If you're paddling on the weekend, expect to see a lot of motorboats. But, there is a lot of wildlife in the channel. Look for stingrays, dolphins, and even sea turtles. Two or three pairs of ospreys have nests on channel markers. If you feel energetic, peel off to the right and explore Sugar Bay.

You approach Goodland at just over 1½ miles from Coon Key. Coon Key Pass narrows considerably, but you enter a manatee zone, slowing boaters to idle speed. As the pass winds past Goodland, you can cut across Goodland Bay if you have enough water. Otherwise, you may need to follow the channel around to the bridge and then cut over to your launch site. Look for least terns diving for minnows in Goodland Bay. In the shadow of the Goodland Bridge, you can see the burned out, collapsed remains of the old wooden drawbridge built in 1936.

3.   *Coon Key and Western Gullivan Bay Islands*

Trip highlights: Beautiful beaches, open bays, dolphins and other marine wildlife

Charts/maps: NOAA Nautical Chart #11430, the waterproof Pasadena Top Spot Fishing Map N-204

Trip rating: Easy

Estimated total time: 4–6 hours

Total distance: 6–7 nautical miles round trip

Hazards: Powerboats, possible strong wind and tide

Launch site: Goodland Bridge

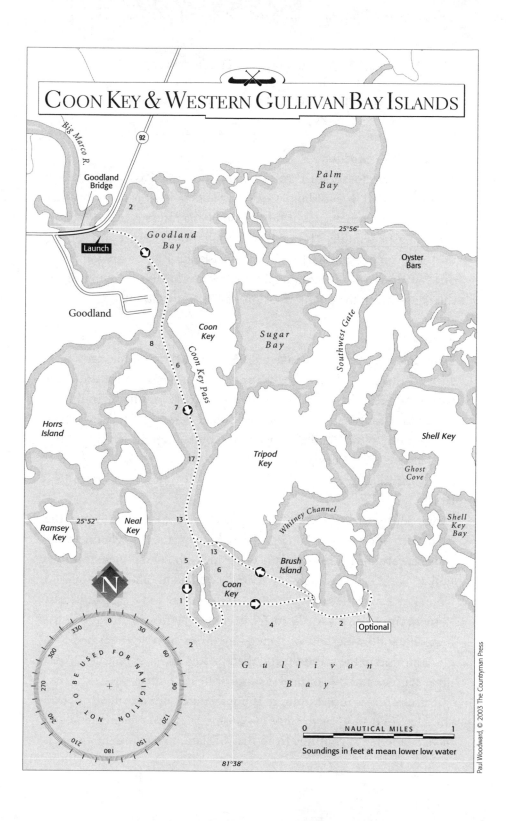

Coon Key & Western Gullivan Bay Islands

Big Marco R.

92

Goodland
Bridge

2

Palm
Bay

25°56'

Goodland
Bay

Launch

5

Oyster
Bars

Goodland

Coon
Key

Sugar
Bay

Southwest Gate

8

6

Coon Key Pass

7

Horrs
Island

17

Tripod
Key

Shell Key

Ghost
Cove

25°52'

Ramsey
Key

Neal
Key

13

Whitney Channel

Shell
Key
Bay

13

5

13

6

Brush
Island

Coon
Key

1

Optional

4

2

N

2

Gullivan

Bay

NOT TO BE USED FOR NAVIGATION

0   NAUTICAL MILES   1

Soundings in feet at mean lower low water

81°38'

> **Ownership:** Rookery Bay National Estuarine Research Reserve
>   (239-417-6310)
> **Alternate routes:** Continue from Brush Island to explore two
>   unnamed islands.

General Information

This is an easy loop tour through busy Coon Key Pass to Coon Key, Tripod Key, and Brush Island. Coon Key Pass in itself is not a thrilling paddle, but you may encounter dolphins, manatees, sea turtles, and other marine wildlife. The scenery is really worth it once you get out into Gullivan Bay and start exploring the islands. Ride an outgoing tide out and return on an incoming tide. Allow for the difference in time of the tide between the mouth of Coon Key Pass and Goodland.

Access

From the town of Marco, take CR 953 (San Marco Boulevard) east, which turns into CR 92, cross over the Goodland Bay Bridge, and then launch on the right side of the road. From US 41 (Tamiami Trail) and the flashing caution light just west of Collier-Seminole State Park, take CR 92 south to the Goodland Bridge and pull off on the left side of the road just before the bridge to launch.

Route

Paddle southeast at about 140 degrees across Goodland Bay toward the eastern tip of Goodland. You may have to follow the boat channel running beneath the bridge and then alongside Goodland if the tide is low. Follow Coon Key Pass southeast from Goodland for about 1½ miles to Coon Key. Enjoy the sandy shoreline of Coon Key and then paddle east ¼ mile across Coon Key Pass to Tripod Key. Mangrove driftwood dominates the southwest shore of Tripod Key. From the beach at Tripod Key, circle around to the south tip and then paddle about ½ mile at 120 degrees southeast to the southwest shore of Brush Key.

Brush Key is nice, but there is not as much interesting driftwood shoreline to explore as the other two islands. If you are energetic and have tide to burn, continue from Brush Island to explore the two un-

Dolphins surfacing in Coon Key Pass

named islands with white sandy beaches just east of Brush Island. Return then to Coon Key Pass and ride an incoming tide back to Goodland Bridge.

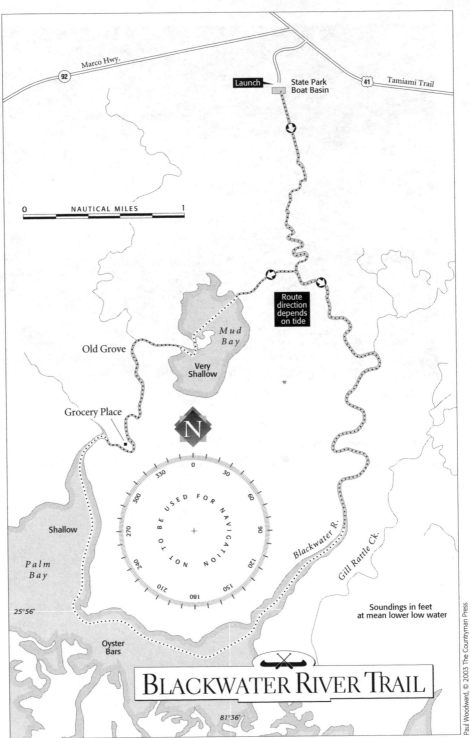

Marco Hwy.

92

41 Tamiami Trail

Launch State Park
Boat Basin

0 NAUTICAL MILES 1

Route
direction
depends
on tide

Mud
Bay

Old Grove

Very
Shallow

Grocery Place

N

330 0 30

300 60

NOT TO BE USED FOR NAVIGATION

270 90

Shallow

240 120

Palm
Bay

210 150

180

25°56'

Blackwater R.

Gill Rattle Ck.

Soundings in feet
at mean lower low water

Oyster
Bars

BLACKWATER RIVER TRAIL

81°36'

Paul Woodward, © 2003 The Countryman Press

PART II
Collier-Seminole State Park

Collier-Seminole State Park is a 6,400-acre park located 8½ miles west of Naples right off US 41 (Tamiami Trail). Named in part for the Seminoles and prominent entrepreneur and developer Barron Collier, who donated land for the park in 1947, Collier-Seminole features an interesting blend of cultural landmarks and natural diversity. Paddlers will be most interested in the 12-mile canoe trail that meanders through a 4,760-acre mangrove wilderness preserve bordering Palm Bay, northern Blackwater Bay, and the Blackwater River.

Other highlights in the park include a large tropical hardwood hammock reminiscent of the coastal forests of the Yucatán and West Indies, one of the historic walking dredges used to construct the Tamiami Trail between Miami and Naples, primitive and developed camping, and mountain bike and hiking trails. Paddlers must file a float plan at the ranger station before launching, and the park limits the number of paddlers on the river at any given time. Canoe rentals are also available at the ranger station. Collier-Seminole State Park can be particularly buggy, so call the ranger station before you arrive to inquire about current conditions.

4. Blackwater River Trail

Trip highlights: Good birding, nice scenery, fishing opportunities
Charts/maps: Waterproof Chart #40E, NOAA Nautical Chart
#11430, trail map provided by park

Trip rating: Moderate
Estimated total time: 5–6 hours
Total distance: 12 nautical miles round trip
Hazards: Shallow, muddy bays at low tide, possible strong wind in
    Palm Bay, motorboats
Launch site: Collier-Seminole Boat Basin
Ownership: Collier-Seminole State Park (239-394-3397)
Alternate routes: None

General Information

The Blackwater River Trail is a long loop trip linking Blackwater River
with northern Blackwater Bay, Palm Bay, a wide unnamed creek, and
Mud Bay. The trip offers nice paddling along a tidal mangrove river and
tidal creeks, as well as shallow bays and mudflats that provide opportunities to see wading birds and shorebirds feeding at lower tide stages.
Grocery Place and Old Grove are of historical interest. Navigating this
route is fairly straightforward and there are a couple of opportunities
to get out and stretch your legs. Channel markers mark your progress
when you are paddling on the Blackwater River portion of the trip.
When you register at the ranger station and file your float plan, a ranger
will probably give you a photocopy map of the canoe route and wilderness preserve. While this is a useful aid, don't rely on it as your sole navigation source.

Access

Follow US 41 south (Tamiami Trail) from the intersection with CR 951
in East Naples for approximately 8½ miles to Collier-Seminole State
Park. The park entrance is located just beyond the flashing yellow light
marking the intersection of US 41 and CR 92. Once you have registered
inside the ranger station at the park entrance, follow the signs on the
park road to the boat basin (a left off the main park road). Rental canoes and the launch site are on the west end of the boat basin.

Route

You begin your trip at the ramp by the rental canoes. This ramp at low
tide may be muddy and frantic with fiddler crabs scuttling toward their

tiny burrows along the shoreline. An infrequently flooded salt marsh surrounds the area west of the boat basin. After launching and paddling out of the boat basin, turn right and proceed south down a straight canal lined on both sides by red mangroves, with occasional pines jutting up beyond the mangroves, indicating higher ground and fresh water. Marker 56 indicates the end of the canal and the beginning of the natural waterway. Continue south to marker 54. About 500 feet down from marker 54, the river narrows and the canopy threatens to close but then it opens up again. You come around a bend in the river and head west toward marker 52 (where a canoe sign points to the left). Continue on a generally south course past marker 51 to marker 49 through alternately narrow and nearly canopied portions of river to slightly wider stretches.

At marker 49, an arrow indicates a sharp left and you head more toward the east. Look carefully among the mangrove roots for gray, square-backed mud crabs. They're shy and will rotate to the side of the root opposite you as you approach, and if that fails, then they'll scuttle up the root to another part of the tree.

The river winds around past marker 48 down to marker 47, which indicates the confluence of the Blackwater River with a creek leading east toward Mud Bay. If you are paddling at low tide, stay to the left and follow the Blackwater River. Continue to the right off the main river down a creek toward Mud Bay only if you are at a higher tide stage. Mud Bay is named for a reason that becomes abundantly clear if you try to traverse it at low tide. Although I was able to get across on a low tide, it was neither easy nor fun and I don't recommend it.

The creek that breaks off Blackwater River heads west to southwest toward Mud Bay and begins as a narrow tunnel that immediately widens and opens up to 50 feet or so. Continue southwest across Mud Bay, skirting either side of a mangrove island in its center, toward the western edge of the bay. On the Collier-Seminole Wilderness Preserve map, the outlet from Mud Bay will be marked as Old Grove. Mud Bay seems shallowest at its center, so if necessary skirt the edges or follow whatever channels you can find going across the center to reach the west side toward Grocery Place. You may see spotted sandpipers, white ibis, and egrets feeding on mudflats. Mud Bay is about 2½ miles from the launch site.

Take the creek west out of Mud Bay. Old Grove will be on your left. At about 3 miles from the boat ramp, the main course of the creek bends sharply to the left, while a feeder creeks trickles away to the right. Stay to the left. You'll head southwest through a section of creek that is broad, shallow, and muddy, with an indistinct mangrove shoreline crowding both sides and sable palms popping above the mangroves here and there.

At a little more than 3½ miles from your launch site, the creek takes another sharp bend right, or west, before heading again southwest. After another ¼ mile or so, you will come upon Grocery Place on your right (west bank of river). Grocery Place makes a good stop to get out and stretch your legs. I believe it also serves as the primitive campsite for overnight stays. During a lower tidal stage, getting out of your boat to go ashore can be a little bit treacherous among the roots and mud because the channel drop-off is abrupt.

From Grocery Place, continue south/southeast before making another sharp turn toward west and then northwest to form a half-loop around Grocery Place. You'll see the remains of what was probably the foundation of a house or store. Just beyond Grocery Place at about 4 miles from the launch site, the creek suddenly widens and turns left or south/southwest. Another much smaller creek wriggles away to the northwest. On your maps, this creek looks as if it loops back to become the little creek you encountered on your right at Grocery Place, but for this route you stay with the main stream heading left. If you are using the Waterproof Chart #40E, this is where you briefly go off the map and if needed must rely on either the park map or preferably your NOAA Nautical Chart #11430.

The main creek, very wide at this point, now actually forms the northern tip of Palm Bay. Stay to the left hugging the east shore and head south toward the southeastern corner of Palm Bay where it connects with Blackwater Bay. You want to stay on this side of the bay to avoid missing the cut that links the two bays. Also, as with Mud Bay, Palm Bay is muddy and shallow at its center. Wind blowing hard out of the south or southwest, particularly on an outgoing tide, causes a heavy chop on the bay and can make this segment of the trip miserable.

About halfway down the length of Palm Bay, you can resume using the Waterproof Chart #40E for navigation. You'll pass a series of little mangrove islands. Stay between these islands and the mainland on your left. At about 5½ miles from your launch site, the bay narrows into a pass and heads east. This is also a good place to see bottle-nosed dolphins. Once in the mouth of the pass, make a sharp left and head east/northeast. Bend to the north and the left shoreline and stay to the left, ignoring the path that leads toward a more open bay to the southeast at about 150 degrees. Stay on a 70-degree course keeping the shoreline on your left. This pass splits into several smaller passes after a short distance. Continue on your 70-degree heading and then adjust your course to head a little more east. This little connecting pass between the bays is only about ¼ mile long. If you somehow stray into one of the other passes, they all lead into Blackwater Bay, and you need only head east across the bay to the channel markers that will bring you back north up the Blackwater River and back on your route. The little pass splinters again, but keep paddling east. The bottom here is littered with oyster bars, meaning that if you like to fish, there should be great opportunities for redfish, snook, sheepshead, and big sea trout.

You'll quickly reach the open water of Blackwater Bay. Willets and other shorebirds are common at this end of Blackwater Bay; and if the tide is high, they'll be concentrated in the drop roots and lower branches of the mangroves dotting the bay. Continue paddling east across the open water at about 110 degrees until you reach the channel markers indicating the mouth of the Blackwater River. At marker 15 you will be heading north beyond the mouth of the Blackwater River and northern Blackwater Bay into the river channel again. Motorboats are common.

You will have traveled about 7 miles at this point. Swallow-tailed kites may be common from this point north up the river anytime from the end of February through the middle of August. At marker 18 a creek comes in from the right. Following this creek (see Waterproof Chart #40E) can take you south into the top of Buttonwood Bay, or if you

Marker 53 on the Blackwater River

follow it north you may eventually hook back into the northern part of the Blackwater River at marker 25 after a more than likely tortuous route through deadfall, spider condos, and overgrown mangrove tunnels. Your safe bet is stick to the main river channel.

You'll arrive at marker 23 just about where the river turns sharply north after a sharp bend west/southwest at just over 8 miles from your starting point. In the spring, crab trap buoys dot the river surface. Paddling another mile brings you to marker 24, and a creek comes in from the north (right) at marker 25 as the river bends west. At 10 miles you reach marker 33 and reenter Collier-Seminole State Park. Listen for prairie warblers singing in the mangroves. Paddling another few hundred yards north reunites you with marker 47, this time pointing straight to keep you on your north course back upriver. This section of river through the park is well-groomed, the mangrove limbs trimmed up, to allow a pontoon tour boat to pass through.

You will have paddled 11½ miles when you reach marker 54 on your return loop and another mile puts you back at the boat basin. There are really no options for shorter loops on this route, although you can paddle to Mud Bay and then back to the boat basin, or follow the main channel of the Blackwater River to Blackwater Bay and return the same way to create a less strenuous tour. If you plan on paddling this route and you are starting out on a low tide, reverse the course set out here by paddling south down the Blackwater River and east across the top of Blackwater Bay, following the flood tide into Palm Bay, and then north and east to Mud Bay to allow water to move back into Palm Bay and Mud Bay.

Mangrove-lined canal

PART III

Port of the Islands

Traveling Tamiami Trail some 20 miles east of Naples, you are jolted by an unlikely apparition rising amid the seemingly limitless expanse of marsh and tree islands whizzing past your car window. No, it's not skunk ape. It's Port of the Islands, a resort complex of single-family homes, condominiums, and townhouses, plus a hotel, restaurant, and marina, perched along both sides of the vast Faka Union Canal. Port of the Islands, originally Remuda Ranch, dates back to the 1950s and was refurbished in 2001 to its current state. Paddlers will find a single concrete boat ramp and small store at the marina just beyond the hotel, in addition to lodging and a restaurant dubbed the Manatee Grill and Bar. The marina charges a modest ramp fee.

The Faka Union Canal was dug in the 1950s along with many smaller canals to help drain the western Everglades for Gulf America Corporation's Southern Golden Gate Estates, slated at 173 square miles to be the world's largest subdivision. Fortunately for the western Big Cypress Swamp, the project went bankrupt and drainage was to some degree ineffective, despite the maze of roads and canals. Most of the land that made up Southern Golden Gate Estates was never developed, and state and federal government agencies have been buying it up for restoration over the last 30 years.

The construction of Faka Union Canal and its feeder canals has not been without environmental consequence, however. In a natural state, fresh water in the Big Cypress Swamp flows through cypress strands and marshes in a wide, shallow sheet toward the mangroves and bays of the 10,000 Islands. In the Southern Golden Gate Estates, however, those small feeder canals shunt fresh water from surrounding wetlands primarily west of Port of the Islands into Faka Union Canal, which rapidly dumps it into Faka Union Bay. This focused discharge of fresh water upsets the delicate brackish balance of this part of the 10,000 Islands by dramatically lowering salinity in Faka Union Bay and raising salinity in bays to the west starved of sheet flow. Hydrologic restoration plans already in progress call for roads and canals in Southern Golden Gate Estates, now Picayune Strand State Forest, to be removed and the flow of Faka Union Canal to be reduced up to 99 percent by means of a redistribution of sheet flow through natural waterways spread out over nearly 20 miles of coastline. For the environment, this restoration will result in a healthier 10,000 Islands estuary. For paddlers, it may mean additional waterways with adequate flow to explore in the future.

Another consequence of all the fresh water flowing down Faka Union Canal is that it has attracted manatees, primarily in the area just below the spillway at the bridge. Manatees need fresh water to drink and the spillway is like a water fountain in a hot city park. Faka Union Canal and the surrounding finger canals throughout Port of the Islands are fairly deep, providing the manatees with a thermal refuge during cold weather. Your chances of seeing a manatee are very good as you set out from the marina, particularly in the winter and early spring when the canal attracts more manatees than anywhere else in the 10,000 Islands. Scientists from Sirenia Project, a division of the U.S. Geologic Survey, as well as the U.S. Fish and Wildlife Service and Rookery Bay National Estuarine Research Reserve, monitor and periodically capture manatees for studies. Some manatees wear GPS tags, which allow researchers to track the manatees' movements by satellite and determine their habitat use and what routes they use to get there. You'll be able to tell which manatees wear transmitters by the small buoy and antenna they tow behind them.

The Faka Union River is the only trip from Port of the Islands covered in this guide, primarily because the Faka Union Canal is long and not particularly exciting. Many people are not even aware that the river exists because they assume the canal obliterated it. There are also several natural mangrove creeks wriggling east from the Faka Union Canal that are ripe for exploration on a day trip. Consider using a local outfitter for a guided trip.

For longer day trips, try the Wood or Little Wood Rivers, which can be reached by paddling the length of the canal into Faka Union Bay and then keeping the shoreline to your right before turning northwest to go upriver. Panther Key, White Horse Key, and Hog Key bordering the Gulf of Mexico offer white sandy beaches worthy of exploration and can be reached by paddling southwest out of Faka Union Bay through Remuda Ranch Channel. The trips to Wood and Little Wood Rivers and the latter mentioned outer islands range from 14–20 miles round trip and should be attempted only by experienced, strong paddlers.

5.   *Faka Union River*

Trip highlights: Exceptional mangrove forest, solitude, diverse habitat, fishing and manatees in Faka Union Canal

Charts/maps: Waterproof Chart #40E

Trip rating: Easy to Moderate

Estimated total time: 8 hours

Total distance: About 11 nautical miles round trip

Hazards: Strong wind and tide possible on Faka Union Canal, possible low water in marsh due to season or tide using alternate route

Launch site: Port of the Islands Marina (239-642-3133; launch fee required)

Ownership: Fakahatchee Strand State Preserve (239-695-4593)

Alternate routes: Leave from US 41 between Bridges 53 and 54, 1 mile east of the Faka Union Canal Bridge, and paddle south through a marsh to connect with the northernmost large lake of the Faka Union River. Follow the lakes and river southwest to the Faka Union Canal and then retrace route upriver.

General Information

This route takes you south down the Faka Union Canal to the Faka Union River. Once on the river you paddle generally northeast and en-

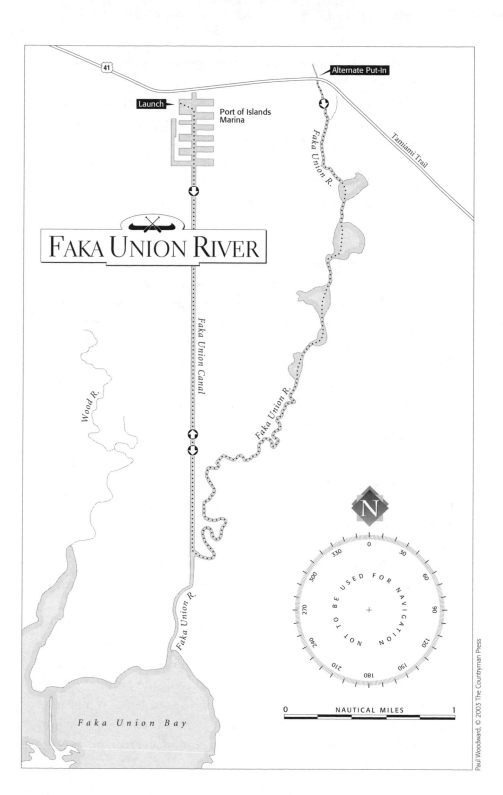

41

Alternate Put-In

Launch

Port of Islands
Marina

Tamiami Trail

Faka Union R.

FAKA UNION RIVER

Faka Union Canal

Wood R.

Faka Union R.

Faka Union R.

Faka Union Bay

N

NOT TO BE USED FOR NAVIGATION

0   30   60   90   120   150   180   210   240   270   300   330

0   NAUTICAL MILES   1

Paul Woodward, © 2003 The Countryman Press

counter beautiful mangrove tunnels, truly impressive old trees, plenty of epiphytic bromeliads and orchids, and then a chain of lakes that eventually leads you to the edge of a marsh within sight of the telephone poles and traffic of US 41. Wildlife is plentiful and may include rare species such as the bald eagle, American crocodile, and mangrove water snake. You return by reversing your direction. You must have the Waterproof Chart #40E to follow this route all the way to the upper lakes and in particular to follow the alternate route starting at US 41.

Access

Port of the Islands is located between Naples and Everglades City just off US 41 (Tamiami Trail). From East Naples, drive east on US 41 southbound just over 13½ miles from the intersection with CR 951. Turn right at the main entrance (before the bridge). The marina is on the left just beyond the hotel. From Everglades City, drive north on FL 29 for 3 miles to US 41. Turn left and drive west on northbound US 41 for 10 miles to Port of the Islands. Turn left at the main entrance on the west side of Faka Union Canal.

Route

Despite the fact that you begin this trip at a marina and must paddle more than 2 miles down Faka Union Canal just to reach the river, there are a wealth of things to see once you get on the water, including tarpon, manatees, and some big gators. If you like to fish, consider trolling as you paddle the canal to spice up the journey. Snook and redfish regularly patrol the edges of the canal. Because of manatees, boats are restricted to slow or idle speed throughout the canal, so there really isn't a hazard due to boat traffic. You'll see plenty of wildlife before you even leave Port of the Islands, including perhaps a pair of bald eagles and vultures breakfasting together on the perfectly manicured lawn of a million-dollar home. Also, you'll see ospreys and dozens of purple martins. Martin houses adorn several backyards along the canal.

You will pass several creeks leading off to your left as you paddle down the canal, including one with a wrecked boat at its mouth. At low tide these may be nothing but an expanse of mud and mangroves. The

Entering a mangrove tunnel

mouth of the Faka Union River lies about 2½ miles from the marina and about ¼ mile before the canal makes a bend toward the southwest. A large buttonwood tree marks the river's mouth on the east shore. As you enter the river, you will pass some wreckage on your left and what looks like the remains of a water monitoring station. The water is surprisingly deep, about 4 feet, even at low tide. Unfortunately, as with most rivers in the 10,000 Islands, you will not be able to escape the whine of airboats in the distance unless it is a rare day.

A mangrove canopy quickly closes over the river, with the mangroves forming a beautiful arch, giving the tunnel a spacious, airy quality. The river is quite serpentine here in its lower half; and it will take you east, then northwest, and then southeast in short order. Your general upriver progress is northeast, however. There are many mangrove crabs in this section of river, and great gangs of them scrabble from the waterline up the mangrove roots like pirates manning the rigging of a sailing ship as you pass by.

Soon you paddle around a bend dominated by really incredible red mangroves that resemble herbivorous dinosaurs craning their necks across the river. Then the canopy breaks and the water becomes more shallow with a hard sand bottom. There are numerous side creeks that often lead to quiet ponds, but stay on the main channel unless you are positive you can find your way back. If the sun is shining, the sand bottom is beautifully illuminated. You'll begin to see more buttonwood trees, many adorned with airplants and orchids.

At about 4 miles into the trip, the river makes a sharp turn west and gives you a choice to go either right or left. Stay to the left. Veering right leads to a dead end after a short distance. Paddle another ½ mile or so to you reach the first of the chain of small lakes that form the upper part of the river. The mangroves in these lakes are generally small and the water is shallow, with plenty of mullet. Continue paddling north to connect with the next lake. Be aware that the lakes will be shallow at low tide. At the northeast corner of the last lake in the chain, you can stand on a firm, almost manicured, grassy shoreline and gaze across a salt marsh pocked with stunted mangroves at the telephone poles along US 41. Look for mullet, ducks, bald eagles, and probably a small gator or two in this lake. At 5½ miles from the marina, you begin your paddle back.

To return, retrace your route southwest through the lakes and into the river. A change in tide may have altered the appearance of the river so that on your return trip the mangrove waterscape will look different than it did a couple hours earlier. You will notice a nice current in the river, so you shouldn't get lost. You'll paddle about 3 miles downriver to reach the confluence with Faka Union Canal and then paddle north another 2½ miles to the marina.

Alternate Route

This is a gorgeous little route you can paddle for its own merit as a short marsh trip or to reach the Faka Union River via the upper chain of lakes. However, parts of the marsh may dry up from March through May; and even if there is water in the marsh, the tide may be out in the lakes and you will still have to portage through muck. You might also have to hunt around for a channel that remains consistently deep

> The abundance of mosquitoes in June…is controlled only by the amount of space there is to hold them. —Archie Carr, *The Everglades*

enough to paddle.

The route starts from US 41, threading its way south through a beautiful marsh with scattered tree islands and following narrow, shallow, braided channels that eventually merge with a more distinct channel. This channel then drops you into the northeast corner of the first big lake (going from north to south) in the Faka Union chain of lakes. It's a particularly nice sunset trip, but don't go at the end of the day until you have paddled it a few times without getting lost.

Launch from the south side of US 41, 1 mile east of the Faka Union Canal Bridge. You launch at an area of open water that spreads into marsh. The water is very shallow and the bottom is silty and soft. This is not a place to get out and walk around. Stand on grassy areas to keep from sinking. Remember you may not make it to the lake without portaging if the tide is out or if you are paddling late in spring.

Paddle south from US 41 and follow a channel of water through the grass. There may be several braids of channel, but choose one that takes a south to slightly southeast direction. In particular, look for deeper water that has current once you get into the main body of the marsh. After 750 feet or so, the channel may shift a little southwest for another 800 feet before continuing south. After ½ mile you come to a tiny tunnel you need to snake through. The channel should have nice current with a hard sand bottom. You may also see aquatic grasses. Mangroves border the creek, and prairie with palmetto heads extends beyond that. Soon there's another tunnel that leads to a big pond. Paddle south across the pond. You should now be in the Faka Union chain of lakes. Head south to continue down the river.

PART IV

Tamiami Trail

Tamiami Trail (US 41) spans the Big Cypress Swamp for more than 60 miles between East Naples and the Miami-Dade county line. The Trail, as it is often called, gets its name from a joining of Tampa and Miami, which is exactly what the road was intended to do and still does today, clogged as it is now by cities, traffic, and stoplights. Initial steps for the construction of Tamiami Trail began in 1915, despite the fact that much of the path the road was to take had never been surveyed or thoroughly investigated and there was only a vague notion of how much it might cost to actually complete it. Dredges from Naples and Miami began digging their way inland toward the interior of the swamp. World War I and a land boom and bust conspired to escalate road-building costs. Money for the road ran out and progress faltered.

In the spring of 1923, a group called the Trail Blazers set out to drive Model T Fords on the unfinished 40-mile gap in the trail between Collier (then Lee) and Dade Counties. It took 11 days with the men walking the last 3½ miles out. Tractors later towed out the Model Ts. Between Carnestown and the Dade County line, the muck bottom gave way to limestone and dynamite was needed by the train-car load to blast the way through. Barron Collier and his new county based in Everglades City bonded most of the rest of the cost for construction until 1926, when the state took over. The Tamiami Trail officially opened at a ceremony in Fort Myers on April 25, 1928.

The opening of Tamiami Trail would prove to alter radically the face of the Big Cypress Swamp and 10,000 Islands in the years that followed. Vegetable farms and their associated communities, focusing primarily on tomatoes, sprang up in Ochopee and Copeland in what had only a few years before been wilderness. A few vegetable and tree farms still operate near the road within the Collier County rural fringe just west of Collier-Seminole State Park. Virtually all of the old-growth pine and cypress in the Big Cypress Swamp was lumbered after the completion of the trail, in part due to the demand for lumber during World War II. The trail is still one of only two east-west roads between Naples and Miami and serves as the primary avenue of entry into Big Cypress National Preserve, the Gulf Coast portion of Everglades National Park, and the towns of Everglades City and Chokoloskee.

Despite the fact that virtually all of the wetlands between Collier-Seminole State Park and west Miami have been set aside for conservation and watershed protection, the Tamiami Trail continues to exact a toll on the environment. The roadbed acts as an earthen dam that restricts the movement of fresh water draining from wetlands on the north side of the trail toward those on the south side, funneling water through only a few narrow channels. Some areas are left starved for fresh water and others receive too much. In late 2003 work began to install 62 additional culverts between Collier-Seminole State Park and the 50-Mile Bend so that water can pass from north to south beneath the trail over a wider area. Twenty earthen plugs will be installed as well to help funnel fresh water through the culverts and into wetlands south of the trail, rather than ushering it through the canal that parallels the north side of the road. The ultimate goal of the $20 million project is that the movement of water passing through the culvert system beneath the trail will more closely resemble the historic sheet flow and hydrologic cycle of the western Everglades and Big Cypress Swamp.

The Tamiami Trail section details seven routes that originate either from the roadside of Tamiami Trail or from Seagrape Drive, the Park Service road running south from the trail, just west of Big Cypress National Preserve headquarters. Another route, the alternate for the Faka Union River tour (refer to Part III), also leaves from the Tamiami Trail roadside. Numerous other waterways, many of them short enough for an hour of exploration within earshot of the road, meander south from the trail as well. This is a good way to enjoy a sunset in the marshes.

Regardless of what route you paddle from Tamiami Trail, use extreme caution when pulling over to the side of the road or unloading your boat and gear. When unloading, keep as far off the road as you can. The traffic between Miami and Naples regularly includes commercial trucks using the trail to dodge tolls on I-75 and business travelers hurrying along at the 60-mph speed limit or greater. Fifteen people have died in traffic accidents on the trail within Big Cypress National Preserve in the last six years, evidence of a serious conflict between business and visitor traffic. Heavy business use may be at odds with the scenic highway designation of this part of the trail and its function as the main access road through the preserve. Big Cypress National Preserve is spending more than $3 million to build wayside areas, parking areas, and deceleration/acceleration lanes that will help, but not solve, a critical problem along this road.

6.   East River

> **Trip highlights:** Beautiful mangrove tunnels, plentiful wildlife, island with shell mound and remains of settlements
> **Charts/maps:** Waterproof Chart #40E, map provided by Fakahatchee Strand State Preserve
> **Trip rating:** Moderate to Difficult
> **Estimated total time:** 7–8 hours
> **Total distance:** 13 nautical miles round trip
> **Hazards:** Alligators, long trip, strong tidal influence on lower river, wind on Fakahatchee Bay, several opportunities to get lost
> **Launch site:** Borrow pond off US 41 in Fakahatchee Strand State Preserve
> **Ownership:** Fakahatchee Strand State Preserve (239-695-4593)
> **Alternate routes:** Mangrove tunnel section

General Information

East River is one of three large rivers that flows from the Fakahatchee Strand, the largest and westernmost of Big Cypress Swamp's major cy-

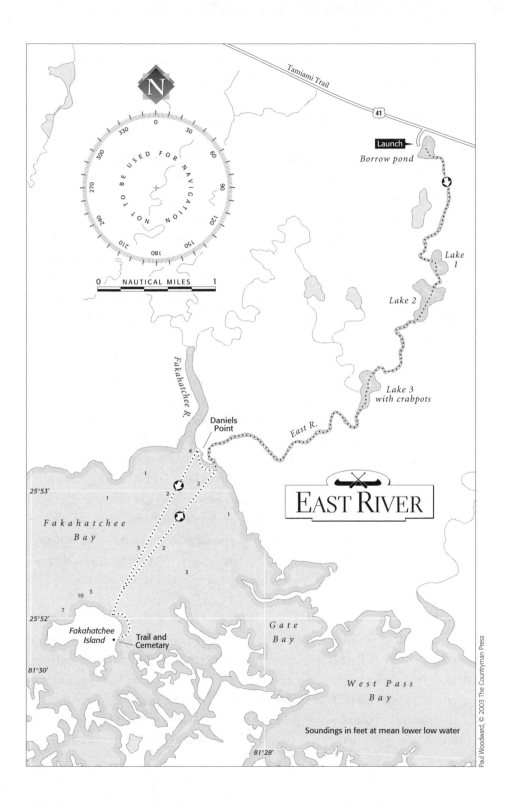

Tamiami Trail

41

Launch
Borrow pond

Lake 1

Lake 2

Lake 3
with crabpots

East R.

Fakahatchee R.

Daniels
Point

4

25°53'

1

1

2

2

2

1

Fakahatchee
Bay

3

2

3

10   3

7

25°52'

81°30'

Fakahatchee
Island

Trail and
Cemetary

Gate
Bay

West Pass
Bay

Soundings in feet at mean lower low water

81°28'

N

NOT TO BE USED FOR NAVIGATION

0   30   60   90   120   150   180   210   240   270   300   330

0   NAUTICAL MILES   1

EAST RIVER

Paul Woodward, © 2003 The Countryman Press

press strands. The other two are the Fakahatchee and Ferguson Rivers. This relatively long route follows the East River as it courses south toward Fakahatchee Bay through a series of sometimes intimate, sometimes majestic, mangrove tunnels broken by quiet small lakes. You then cross Fakahatchee Bay to Fakahatchee Island, a large midden island rich with tropical hardwoods and steeped in human history. You may see a rare American crocodile or white-crowned pigeon on this trip, in addition to large alligators.

Given that the East River route includes both intimate, narrow mangrove tunnels and a wide bay to cross, I don't suggest a short river kayak because of the open water involved. A kayak or canoe 14–16 feet long is ideal. Anything longer than 16 feet tends to get hung up in the smaller tunnels. If you want a shorter trip, paddle only the mangrove tunnel section of the river, turning back when you reach the point where the river becomes much wider as it nears Fakahatchee Bay. For a short trip of this nature, a diminutive kayak of 9–14 feet or so is ideal and a lot of fun. I also use a break-apart kayak paddle for this route because there are sections where the mangrove tunnels are too narrow to allow me to use the full paddle. Some kayakers prefer to lash a short canoe paddle to their bow to use when paddling these narrow tunnels.

There is one important thing you should know about this trip before you decide to paddle it. The mangroves here are full of long-jawed orb weaver spiders that often spin their webs to span the distance across a tunnel. The spiders are beautiful, completely harmless, and typically drop into your boat or onto your hat if you paddle through a web. I have never had one bite me. Gently help them back over the side into the mangroves. If you have a spider phobia, this may not be the trip for you.

Access
Follow US 41 south (which is east) about 18 miles from its intersection with CR 951 in East Naples. Your indication to slow down for the right turn from US 41 onto the unmarked gravel drive leading to the launch site is a small wayside park, also on the right, less than ¼ mile before the turn. If you are driving west from Everglades City, Miami, or Ft. Lauderdale, the turn is just over 5 miles west of the intersection of FL

A cistern on Fakahatchee Island

29 and US 41 on the south (left) side of the road. Follow the short gravel drive to the edge of the pond to launch. Parking is extremely limited, so you may need to park along the side of US 41 after unloading.

Route

Launch your boat at the large pond formed by the removal of fill material used to build the raised bed for US 41. Head southeast across the pond toward the south corner, where you'll find a small cut in the mangroves on your right barely large enough to get a boat through. Rangers from Fakahatchee Strand State Preserve periodically flag the route you will follow, including this entrance, but folks who consider flags an eyesore and a crutch for people who shouldn't be there generally tear them down in short order. Once in the cut, paddle through a short mangrove tunnel that leads to an opening and then curve to the left through another tiny tunnel before popping out into the first long pond, which I believe is actually a canal. Turn right and head south down the pond. You'll see saw grass prairie and big leather ferns behind the mangrove border on your right. After about ½ mile, you reach the end of the pond. Bear slightly to the left into a short tunnel, which takes you into another little opening with prairie and leather ferns to your left. With the prairie on your left, paddle into the small tunnel almost directly in front of you, staying to your right. If this isn't marked and you have trouble finding the opening, watch where the water flows and look for branches that seem to have been deliberately broken. You are now in the first of the long tunnels, during which time you will probably lose reception if you are using a GPS. Paddle until you reach a small pond and then a second larger one. This larger pond is Lake 1 on the park map and indicates you are about 1½ miles from the canoe launch. It will be the northernmost of the chain of lakes you see after the canal on your Waterproof Chart #40E.

Head south to southeast across the pond until it narrows, and then you will enter another mangrove tunnel. You'll notice the character of this tunnel is different from the last one you went through. The canopy is higher and there is a profusion of bromeliads (airplants), including Spanish moss. After a few minutes, the tunnel dead-ends into what I call the T, marked by a giant buttonwood tree festooned with airplants. Turn left. There may be a couple of places in this tunnel that you need to portage due to downed mangroves, but it's unlikely. You will pass through a curtain of mangrove drop roots and the tunnel will twist and turn for ½ mile or so. Your bearing coming out of this tunnel is about 240 degrees to cross Lake 2 and find the opening to the tunnel on the other side.

This third major tunnel is the longest and winds southwest for 1 mile or so to what the state park calls Big Lake. The tunnel canopy is higher, the water is deeper, and the bottom is very muddy. If the tide has dropped, you may be paddling 1 or 2 feet below the stained mangrove roots and mud bank at the edge of the river. Notice the pneumatophores of the black mangroves, which rise from the mud like dark snorkels and help aerate the trees' root systems. This is extraordinary mangrove forest, with red mangroves at the edges and black mangroves farther back. The pneumatophores extend all the way to the riverbank, punctuated here and there with dead, brightly colored yellow-and-orange red mangrove leaves. You could also see white ibis, red-shoul-

Striped mullet

The striped mullet *(Mugil cephalus)* is the fish you see making a seemingly random series of two, three, or even four leaps as high as 3 feet out of the water as you paddle wide rivers or shallow areas near shore. Occasionally one joins you in your boat. They are a vital part of the estuarine food web in the 10,000 Islands and a smoked delicacy you can find in local fish shops at Everglades City. Striped mullet are also known as black or gray mullet. The mullet family *(Mugilidae)* is a circumtropical family of more than 100 species common to warm fresh water, estuarine areas, and offshore habitats. Striped mullet are dark bluish-gray along the upper part of the body, with silver sides, whitish undersides, and a series of dark stripes that run the length of the body. Research shows they may live from 5–25 years, attain more than 2 feet in length, and weigh several pounds.

Striped mullet range in the western Atlantic from Brazil to Nova Scotia, in the Caribbean, and in the Gulf of Mexico. Adults gather in large schools in the fall and migrate from shallow estuarine areas to offshore spawning grounds from October to February, although they remain common in the 10,000 Islands year-round. Striped mullet spawn offshore near the surface, and females lay eggs within 48 hours of fertilization. Larvae hatch offshore along the continental shelf and are distributed by currents. They remain among plankton for two to three months. Striped mullet larvae form dense schools when they are just under an inch long and move into inshore waters. They spend most of their first year in shallow estuaries and mature after about three years. As young, they rely on small crustaceans and zooplankton. They are vegetarians as adults, feeding primarily on detritus (decaying bits of plant matter) and algae they suck up through bottom sediments or floating material at the water's surface. Apparently they relish swarming congregations of marine worms when they find them as well.

Mullet are an important food staple for virtually every fish-eating predator in the 10,000 Islands from bald eagles to bull sharks. Because mullet feed on detritus, they are an important link between the inner strands of the food web, such as the microscopic organisms involved in the breaking down of mangrove leaves to form detritus, and organisms living on the outer edges that feed on mullet, including bottle-nosed dolphins, ospreys, and people.

The question that arises among most people regarding mullet is "Why do they jump?" Theories abound, few based on any real research, and offer up such conclusions as they jump to rid themselves of parasites, they are thermoregulating, they are frightened by a predator, they are clearing their gill rakers, or they are jumping for joy. I prefer the latter theory, or lest I be accused of anthropomorphism, I contend they leap so beautifully simply because they can.

dered hawks, and mullet in this tunnel. One section near the end of the tunnel is straight and wide like a boulevard.

You emerge from this tunnel into Big Lake, which on your Waterproof Chart #40E is shaped much like a bladder, and continue paddling south to southwest. The lake is shallow with extensive mud banks and crab trap buoys. On one of my trips, I hit this lake at low tide and encountered a huge gator on a mud bank. I could not back up in time and we nearly collided as he skittered across the mud and extremely shallow water in his attempt to reach the deeper refuge over which I was paddling. I drifted a little, collecting my wits, and then he popped up beside me, not knowing I was there, and the water exploded again as he dove, mullet scattering all around.

As you near the southwestern end of the lake, you'll see a little lagoon to your right, which leads to a series of mangrove tunnels that eventually connect with the Fakahatchee River to your west. Crocodiles are occasionally seen in this part of the lake. Continue south through the narrows of the lake and on to the main wide channel of the East River and this last leg to Fakahatchee Bay. If you're here at low tide, you may have to hunt around for a channel, where the main flow of water is going through the lake, and then continue downriver. Try keeping to the west side. Big Lake marks your turnaround point if you prefer the shorter trip that features only the mangrove tunnels and these lakes.

There are numerous mud bars along the river as well. This is a good area to see spotted sandpipers and occasionally greater yellowlegs sandpipers. Stay in the main river channel and try to avoid getting too close to the mud bars, particularly coming around a bend. I try to scan ahead with binoculars to pick out alligators on the bars. The alligators in this area are not accustomed to people, and when they see you, they race for the water. It may look as if they're charging you, but they're not; they're only trying to reach the safety of the water. Give them a wide berth and both of you will be less frightened. The deepest water in the channel seems to be on its west edge or right side.

The river will soon narrow as it makes a jog to the west, but the canopy does not close. The mud is firm enough on a low tide to get out if needed at the bend where the river turns back south. At about 3¾ miles you will see a little channel going off to your left. This leads to a shallow lake with no apparent outlet. At 4¾ miles you begin to see oyster bars on the banks of the river, indicating your approach to the mouth of East River, Fakahatchee Bay, and Daniels Point. East River is headed west to southwest at this point. Just before you reach the mouth, the river makes an abrupt shift to the south and then southeast. If you have enough water, you can cut through inlets between oyster bars to reach Fakahatchee Bay, rather than follow the main channel out. The mouth of East River is about 5 miles from the canoe launch.

To find Daniels Point after reaching the bay, turn abruptly northwest and keep the shoreline to your right. Paddle about ¼ mile. Daniels Point is an old shell mound with a shallow slope, ideal for beaching a boat, situated at the mouth of the Fakahatchee River. There's nothing really to explore, but it's a good place to get out and stretch your legs if needed before heading across the bay to Fakahatchee Island. There also may be voracious hordes of no-see-ums awaiting your arrival.

Settlers of European descent occupied Fakahatchee Island as early as 1870. Several families farmed it and fished the surrounding waters. In 1912 a school with 13 pupils was established, although there was never a store on the island. Members of the Daniels family lived on Fakahatchee Island into the 1960s. Set your course for 210 degrees and paddle just under 1 mile to reach Fakahatchee Island from Daniels Point. The island will have a distinctive hump-shaped silhouette against the bay because of the large Calusa shell mound. This course should lead you to a place on the island where you can pull up your boat and look at a cistern and shell mound covered with gumbo limbo trees. Be prepared for mosquitoes and no-see-ums throughout the island. Watch out for the barbed wire cactus here. To reach another landing site and visit the trail and little cemetery, paddle east around the island just past the pilings. You'll notice lots of tropical hardwoods, several areas of thorny succulent plants and exotic plants, which indicate previous settlement, and the fenced cemetery. Keep an eye out for shy white-crowned pigeons. Please respect the trees and the historical remains. Take nothing (other than pictures), leave nothing, and carve nothing.

If you want to paddle around Fakahatchee Island, it adds about 2 miles to your trip. You'll follow a compass bearing of about 40 degrees from the cistern to find your way to the mouth of the East River and reverse your course back to the launch point. If you have enough water once you reach the river, you can paddle oxbow to oxbow (point to point) to save a little distance. Don't be surprised if your surroundings look different as you paddle the return route. Although you are covering the same water, the tide has changed and that alters the landscape and the appearance of landmarks somewhat. You may see tarpon rolling at a high tide stage in the wide, lower river. Brace yourself going across the ponds because mullet will explode under your boat and inevitably startle you. Often they fling themselves completely clear of the water and occasionally wind up in the boat.

At Big Lake, a bearing of 30 degrees should lead you to the mangrove tunnel. Paddle through the tunnel to Lake 2. As you emerge at Lake 2, follow a course of 60 degrees across to the next tunnel entrance. It may or may not be marked with flagging tape. Paddle through the tunnel and back through the bead curtain of red mangrove drop roots to the T and large buttonwood tree. Turn right (a nest of roots eventually blocks your path if you try to go straight) and head north.

As you emerge from this tunnel into Lake 1, continue north. As you cross the lake and then enter the second little opening, keep to the right and head straight so you don't miss the tunnel opening. If you do miss it, it's easy to backtrack and find. When you come again to an opening in the tunnel, stay to the left and continue up the tunnel. If you head out to the open area it very shortly becomes a dead end. You should be able to hear road noise from US 41 midway through this tunnel if the wind isn't blowing hard. As you exit the tunnel, head 20 degrees north straight to the connector tunnel that takes you to the long pond (canal). Paddle north about ½ mile. Once you pass the little bay on your right, start looking on your left for the flagging tape that marks the tunnel

---

In meeting the ecologic challenge of life in the difficult, storm-wracked unstable zone where tidal salt water laps the edge of the land, the red mangrove has evolved into one of the most bizarre of all vegetables.
—Archie Carr, *The Everglades*

that takes you back to the borrow pond and your launch point. Once you exit the connector tunnel, head northwest 315 degrees, keeping the little island to your right, to reach the boat launch. If you like to fish, the mangrove shoreline rimming this pond is full of snook and small tarpon.

7. *Fakahatchee River*

Trip highlights: Solitude, beautiful old mangroves at the lower end of the creek near the open water, black-crowned night herons at upper end

Charts/maps: Waterproof Chart #40E

Trip rating: Extremely Difficult (requires endurance and superior navigation skills)

Estimated total time: 9–10 hours

Total distance: About 7 nautical miles round trip

Hazards: Lots of deadfall, overgrown tunnels, numerous chances to get lost

Launch site: Weaver Station on south side of US 41, across from Big Cypress Bend Boardwalk

Ownership: Fakahatchee Strand State Preserve (239-695-4593)

Alternate routes: Return up the East River

General Information

This is the roughest route in this guide. Much like East River a couple miles to the east, Fakahatchee River begins as a series of canopied mangrove creeks that combines to form a wide lower river emptying into Fakahatchee Bay. Unlike the more groomed and traveled East River, Fakahatchee River's mangrove tunnels are more numerous, convoluted, overgrown, and thick with deadfall. The route detailed here follows the central of the three creeks feeding the Fakahatchee River. Outward Bound is said to travel this route every couple years or so, which is probably the only reason you can make it through at all. Do not think this trip will be fun unless you relish returning scratched up, hot, completely covered in spider webs, and thoroughly exhausted.

Do not travel this route unless you are experienced in Everglades

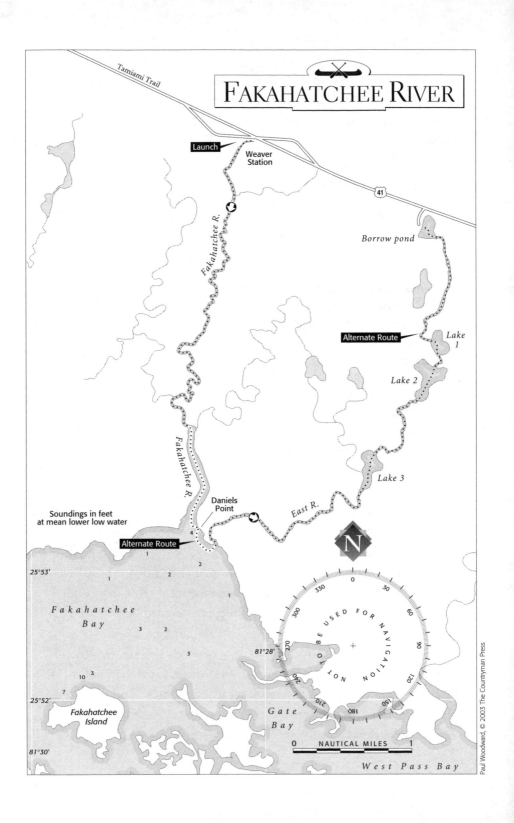

FAKAHATCHEE RIVER

Tamiami Trail

Launch

Weaver Station

41

Fakahatchee R.

Borrow pond

Alternate Route

Lake 1

Lake 2

Lake 3

Fakahatchee R.

East R.

Daniels Point

Soundings in feet
at mean lower low water

Alternate Route

25°53'

Fakahatchee Bay

81°28'

10

7

25°52'

Fakahatchee Island

81°30'

Gate Bay

N

NOT TO BE USED FOR NAVIGATION

0   NAUTICAL MILES   1

West Pass Bay

paddling, and by all means, do not travel this route if you are uncomfortable with being lost. You invariably will get lost, and you have to know how to get yourself either back on track or back out safely. It will be difficult for anyone to rescue you. There are many rivers detailed in this guide that have better scenery and on which you'll see more wildlife. About the only reasons to travel this gnarly route are for the solitude, which is nice (except for the frequent tour plane overflights), and because it's there.

The Fakahatchee River route begins at Weaver Station and claws its way south for 3½ miles or so to the wide lower Fakahatchee River and Daniels Point. You average less than 1 knot per hour, which means you could probably walk faster. Expect to be whipped, thrashed, slashed, smashed, and otherwise similarly abused. If you decide upon reaching Daniels Point that you have suffered enough, you can paddle up the East River (as I did due to impending darkness) and then either walk the 1¾ miles back to Weaver Station to get your vehicle or leave another vehicle at the East River canoe launch.

Use short paddles and a small boat that is 9 or 10 feet long, certainly no longer than 14 feet, because some of the turns are so sharp that a larger craft can't make them without extraordinary effort on your part. Don't forget to bring more than one compass, your chart, plenty of water, and food. A GPS may help you find your way back out if you get turned around and can't continue onward, but do not rely on it as a substitute for chart and compass.

Access

Follow US 41 south (which is east) about 16¾ miles from its intersection with CR 951 in East Naples. Look for the sign for Big Cypress Bend and the Indian village on the left side of the road, and turn right onto the paved road where an old gas station used to be. A two-track path may or may not be visible, depending on tall grass, and leads to a grove of palms and Australian pines. The launch site is at the canal among the pines. If you are driving west from Everglades City, Miami, or Ft. Lauderdale, the turn is just under 7 miles west of the intersection of FL 29 and US 41 on the south (left) side of the road.

Route

Start by heading south down the canal. Within 100 feet or so, you pass through a short, very low tunnel and then come out into a wider part of the canal bordered by black needle rush and cattails on the left and mangroves on the right. This first tunnel is a taste of what to expect for the rest of the trip, and if this does not appeal to you, you should probably turn around. Australian pines and Brazilian pepper rise up beyond the mangroves on the upper part of the canal. Both of these are invasive exotic species that are being eliminated from south Florida parks wherever possible. The bottom of the canal is silty and shallow, with very little flow and copious quantities of algae. The canal eventually bends to the east and then back southwest before beginning to wriggle as it turns into an actual river. You'll pass a single Australian pine surrounded by marsh as you turn to the southwest at about ⅓ mile (10 minutes) into your trip. As you pass the tree, stay to your right. The course to the left leads to a dead end. This is a good place to hear clapper rails and see lots of yellow bladderwort floating at the edge of

A black mangrove on Fakahatchee River

the canal. They are carnivorous, sporting a pretty flower on top and tiny bladders beneath the water that suck in minute aquatic organisms.

At just beyond ½ mile, you pass through a very short mangrove tunnel and then into a pond among the mangroves. Now you are on the river itself. This is a good place to see herons, including black-crowned night herons, great blue herons, and tricolored herons. You'll also notice the white chalky stains on the leaves left by roosting wading birds.

Please remember on this route to take your time. As soon as you gain the slightest amount of speed, something looms ahead to bring you to a swift, typically painful, stop. In many places you will have to pull yourself through with your hands, so if you have a rudder on your boat, you can steer with that as you pull yourself along.

Continue south through the pond to the next tunnel. From this point you paddle through an emerald necklace of short mangrove tunnels and openings in the mangroves. Be prepared for all the spiders that will drop into your boat as you tear through their webs. As with the East River, these spiders are mostly long-jawed orb weavers. Please help them gently back over the side of your boat. They don't bite. After another ⅓ mile you come to a slightly larger pond with mangroves on all sides and possibly more night herons. Paddle southwest through this pond. Candy coral, which looks like silly string or skinny white worms, starts to show up on the red mangrove roots at just under 1 mile into your trip. This is a true coral found in fresh to brackish water.

At just over 1 mile into the trip, you pop out of a short, tight tunnel and then take a sharp left toward the southeast. There is a sandy hump here bordered by marsh on the left that you may have to portage if the water level is low. At any rate, it offers an opportunity to get out of your boat, stretch, and survey your surroundings. Once over the hump you take another sharp turn to the right or southwest into another tunnel. Soon you'll pop out of the tunnel and head straight southeast at about 140 degrees to hit the next tunnel. You'll see an opening to your left. Don't go there because it's a dead end into a spartina marsh.

After another ⅕ mile or so, you reach a beautiful area filled with bromeliads, including a giant arch of a mangrove adorned with these beautiful plants. Continue paddling through another couple openings.

You'll soon come to a little tunnel by downed mangroves. Turn right. Do not continue straight into the other opening through the mangroves that takes you due east. You come to still another opening. The clearest way looks to the left, but instead head right through the mangroves and you'll continue through a tunnel.

At about 1⅓ miles you reach another pond and then turn left back south. Continue south through more tunnels and ponds. Some of the tunnels through this section are dead on the right side, either blasted by a hurricane or killed by frost. The dead mangroves allow a lot of sunlight to come in. At about 1½ miles you reach an open area with spartina marsh on the left and mangroves on the right. Continue almost due north, keeping the spartina marsh on the left, and then pick up a tunnel again to the right. This last turn is extraordinarily tight, and because we had longer boats, we had to really rock our boats to get around it. A few hundred feet farther, you reach another marsh in front of you. Veer right toward the marsh, go maybe 100 feet or so, and pick up the tunnel in front of you. Do not continue into the marsh on the right. You'll paddle through this tunnel and then be faced with an opening directly in front of you. Make a sharp left to continue in the tunnel.

At about 1⁶⁄₁₀ miles you pop out into a clearing with cattails, more spartina, and small dead mangroves in front of you. Turn immediately left to head primarily east. The tunnel that you are in now will be longer than some of the other tunnels so far on this route and after winding around will drop you into still another opening. When you reach this opening, veer slightly to the left and continue into another tunnel. You'll pass more shattered mangrove skeletons, including a hollowed, multi-branched stump. At about 1¾ miles you reach a big cut mangrove log at an opening. Here, turn left (south) under a large mangrove arch. There is a significant snag you will have to shimmy around in the tunnel.

Beyond this point, the character of the mangrove forest begins to change. The trees and the tunnels grow larger. You start to see more black mangroves. You also notice a more pronounced current and the water gets deeper. You soon pop into another opening with more mangrove skeletons and lots of dead wood on the river bottom. As you continue, the river becomes more scenic. The canopy opens up here and there, and you notice more black mangrove pneumatophores. At 1¾ miles the river seems to flow more to the southeast, as you continue through more tunnels, and it is more evidently tidal.

You see high tide marks on the trees and can gauge the progress of the tide by the amount of mud on the banks of the river. You see obvious cuts where someone has been through before, and you may have to pull yourself over numerous logs, depending on tide. Lower water may find you as much as 4 feet below the bank. At one point in this section, my companion and I had to climb out of our kayaks on an outgoing tide, haul the boats over a downed large log suspended over 8 feet of water, and then climb back in. We also lost satellite reception on our GPS unit for more than an hour under the canopy.

The tunnel gradually grows wider as it approaches the open water of the lower Fakahatchee River. I consider this portion of the river the most scenic. The mangroves are immense and the atmosphere is almost parklike. If the current stops it's probably because you have encountered slack tide. The creek is about 20 feet wide at this point and more than 8 feet deep. The creek wriggles in a generally south direction, vacillating from southeast to southwest, until finally making an abrupt turn west a few hundred feet before you encounter the wide water of the lower Fakahatchee River. The main course of the lower river will then revert to a south/southeast course as you paddle slightly more than 1 mile to Daniels Point. Like the East River, there are numerous mud banks to avoid, so keep as best you can to the channel. To return, reverse your course back upriver, or if you think you may run out of daylight or good weather, paddle back up the East River.

When one has been at work in the keys…for a week his body and limbs are filled with thorns of every description, and there is scarcely a spot on him that is not bitten by insects. A man who can endure all this and never lose his temper is fit to be a king; he can govern himself and he should be able to govern others. —Charles Torrey Simpson, *In Lower Florida Wilds*

8.   *Halfway Creek to Everglades City*

Trip highlights: Mangrove tunnels, overall excellent scenery
Charts/maps: Waterproof Chart #40E, Halfway Creek Canoe Trail map provided by Big Cypress National Preserve
Trip rating: Easy
Estimated total time: 5–6 hours
Total distance: About 6½ nautical miles one way
Hazards: Possible moderate current going through mangrove tunnels, stronger current and powerboats near the causeway bridge
Launch site: Seagrape Drive or Everglades National Park canoe ramp
Ownership: Big Cypress National Preserve (239-695-4111)
Alternate routes: None

General Information

Halfway Creek is a beautiful creek bordered by freshwater vegetation near its headwaters and then grading into mangrove habitat as you paddle south. It is among the prettiest creeks in the 10,000 Islands. Gorgeous, large buttonwood trees filled with bromeliads and a few orchids are common at its upper end. This is a marked, well-maintained canoe route that begins at the man-made Seagrape Canal and then follows Halfway Creek down its entire length through mangrove tunnels and past the community of Plantation Island to the canoe ramp at Everglades National Park. Leave a vehicle at the ranger station or arrange for shuttle service from a local outfitter to make this an easy one-way trip from Seagrape Drive.

Tide may dictate which direction you prefer to run this route, although the current you encounter is not as strong as some other areas of the park. Paddle south from Seagrape Drive on an outgoing tide or start from Everglades National Park canoe ramp and paddle north up the creek on an incoming tide.

Access

Travel east on US 41 (Tamiami Trail) about 2½ miles from the inter-

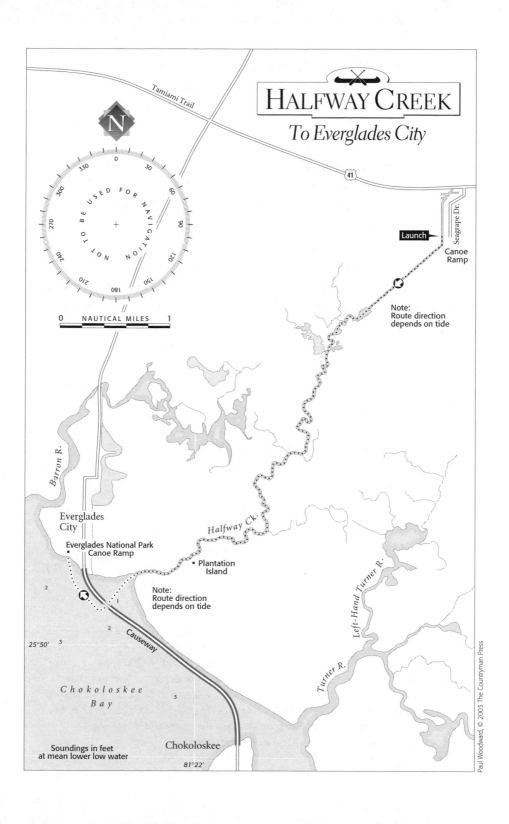

HALFWAY CREEK

To Everglades City

Tamiami Trail

41

Launch

Seagrape Dr.

Canoe Ramp

Note:
Route direction depends on tide

N

NOT TO BE USED FOR NAVIGATION

0 30 60 90 120 150 180 210 240 270 300 330

NAUTICAL MILES

0   1

Barron R.

Everglades City

Everglades National Park Canoe Ramp

Plantation Island

Halfway Ck.

Note:
Route direction depends on tide

Left-Hand Turner R.

2

1

2

3

25°50'

Causeway

Turner R.

Chokoloskee Bay

3

Soundings in feet at mean lower low water

Chokoloskee

81°22'

Paul Woodward, © 2003 The Countryman Press

section of US 41 and FL 29. Turn right on Seagrape Drive, just before you reach Big Cypress National Preserve headquarters. Follow Seagrape Drive about ½ mile until it dead-ends at the canoe launch.

Route

Launch from the canoe ramp and paddle about 1 mile down the man-made Seagrape Canal. As with most canals, this one is straight, with nary a wiggle, and you can see a variety of freshwater shrubs and cattails mixed with mangroves along the bank. The bank provides a good view of the limestone bedrock that underlies all of southern Florida. Look closely to find fossil shells and corals imbedded in the rock.

Shortly after you leave the ramp, you pass a marker on the left for a series of old airboat trails leading away to the east. You no doubt will hear the roar of airboats from the adventure park just to the west. Airboats do not travel into any part of this route, so you don't need to keep an eye out for them.

Seagrape Canal empties into a small nameless lake, the headwaters of Halfway Creek. Palms line the lake beyond the mangroves. Look south across the lake for the first PVC marker of the canoe trail. Halfway Creek keeps a gentle south to southwest course for most of its length. Follow the creek as it meanders past marker 2 to marker 3. The small creek that leads away to the right ties into the Barron River. Continue paddling straight to remain on Halfway Creek. Halfway Creek alternately narrows and widens into small lakes as you paddle down to marker 6, where the canopy begins to close to a tunnel. Continue paddling south to marker 7, almost 2¾ miles from the canoe launch. You may see another marker (1L) identifying the right turn to join the new Halfway Creek/Barron River Loop.

Over the channels great mangroves arch, dimming the sun's glare to soft twilight beneath. Air roots everywhere descend into the channels so completely obstructing the passage that we had frequently to chop our way through....Here and there a great courida (*Avicennia*) towers above the mangroves; the ground beneath being thickly covered with erect quills or pneumatophores, the curious growth from the roots of this tree.
—Charles Torrey Simpson, *In Lower Florida Wilds*

Continue past this junction, following Halfway Creek as it swings sharply east and then south before finally reverting to its lazy southwest course near marker 8. Try not to gain too much speed paddling through the tunnel because you may have to duck in places to slide under overhanging limbs or scoot around fallen trees. It is more than ¾ mile to marker 9, near the junction of Halfway Creek and Left-Hand Turner River. Left-Hand Turner leads away to the east toward Turner Lake. Follow Halfway Creek west as it alternately widens into ponds and then narrows again to canopied creek. The tunnel ends and Halfway Creek widens as you near Plantation Island to the left, leaving Everglades National Park. You also begin to see signs of invasive exotic vegetation, such as Australian pine and Brazilian pepper. Hidden somewhere in the mangroves are cisterns and other remains of old homesteads. Paddle past Plantation Island out to the little bay at the mouth of the creek.

A stiff-leaved wild pine in bloom on a buttonwood branch along Halfway Creek

Stay to the southwest to pass under the causeway bridge. The tide can really rip through here, and if you arrive at low tide, stay in the boat channel on your route to the bridge. After you pass under the bridge, turn to the right and head northwest toward the brown ranger station buildings and the Everglades National Park canoe ramp.

9.   *Halfway Creek/Barron River Loop*

Trip highlights: Beautiful Halfway Creek, mangrove tunnels, overall excellent scenery

Charts/maps: Waterproof Chart #40E, preserve map of Loop L1–L15

Trip rating: Difficult

Estimated total time: 5–6 hours

Total distance: 8½ nautical miles round trip

Hazards: Possible strong current going through mangrove tunnel from Halfway Creek, difficult navigation

Launch site: Seagrape Drive

Ownership: Big Cypress National Preserve (239-695-4111)

Alternate routes: None

General Information

This loop route is one of the prettiest you will paddle in Big Cypress Swamp, but up until the national preserve marked it, it was also one of the toughest to navigate. Halfway Creek/Barron River Loop is now an official canoe trail and 15 PVC markers have been placed along the entire loop. The park may come up with its own name for this route and the loop may be much easier to navigate than its difficult rating suggests because it has been marked, but for now this is how things stand. Contact the preserve for a copy of their trail map, currently called Loop L1–L15, which is actually a colorized aerial.

The route begins innocently enough on the Halfway Creek Canoe Trail (for which there is another useful map provided by the park service), but then it leaves the creek after a couple of miles and enters a mangrove tunnel that winds west into one of the upper lakes of the Barron River. You then follow a creek that travels north from the Barron

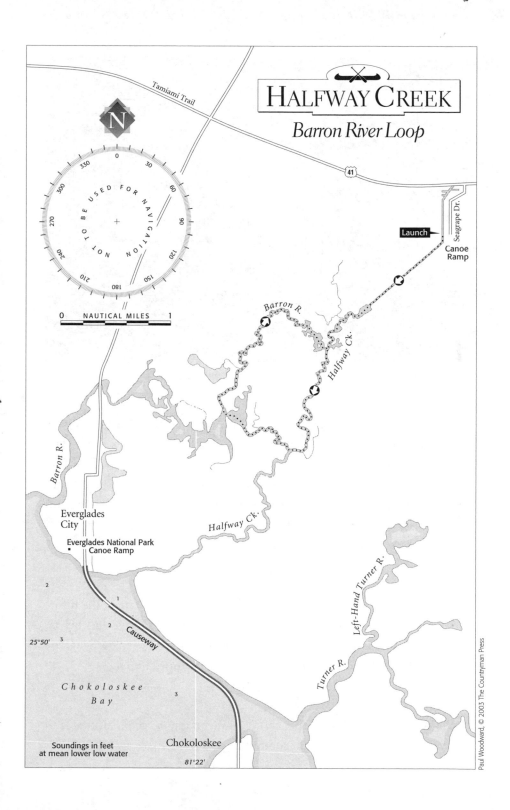

HALFWAY CREEK

Barron River Loop

N

NOT TO BE USED FOR NAVIGATION

0   NAUTICAL MILES   1

Tamiami Trail

41

Launch

Seagrape Dr.

Canoe Ramp

Barron R.

Halfway Ck.

Everglades City

Everglades National Park
Canoe Ramp

Halfway Ck.

Barron R.

Left-Hand Turner R.

Turner R.

Causeway

25°50'

Chokoloskee Bay

Chokoloskee

Soundings in feet
at mean lower low water

81°22'

Paul Woodward, © 2003 The Countryman Press

David Herraden coming around a bend nearing Halfway Creek

River and then southeast to rejoin Halfway Creek at marker 3. Halfway Creek and the Seagrape Canal lead you back to the canoe ramp. The landscape is varied, including majestic buttonwoods along scenic Halfway Creek, mangrove tunnels, prairie and narrow creeks lined with cabbage palms, and wide bays. Surprisingly, there is tidal current up here, so try to time your trip to catch the last of the outgoing tide, about 3 hours after low tide in Everglades City.

Access
Travel east on US 41 (Tamiami Trail) about 2½ miles from the intersection of US 41 and FL 29. Turn right on Seagrape Drive, just before you reach Big Cypress National Preserve headquarters. Follow Seagrape Drive about ½ mile until it dead-ends at the canoe launch.

Route
Paddle down Seagrape Canal about 1 mile, passing an old airboat trail exiting the canal on the left soon after you leave the canoe ramp. The

limestone walls of the canal are representative of the bedrock that underlies all of Big Cypress Swamp and the Everglades. You'll come to a
little lake, which is the headwaters of Halfway Creek. Paddle south toward the white marker. At marker 2 you see a little teaser creek winding
off to the right, but it really doesn't go anywhere. Another feeder creek
wanders off to the left at marker 3. Just past marker 3 on the right is
where you will reconnect with Halfway Creek on your return loop.
Continue paddling south past markers 4 and 5 as you enjoy the beauty
and tranquility of Halfway Creek.

About 2½ miles into your trip, Halfway Creek begins to narrow.
The mangroves crowd from both sides and you see arthritis vine and
candy coral. The canopy soon closes over to form a tunnel. Marker 7
lies another ¼ mile downstream. Turn right into the tunnel leading
away from marker 7. It may also now bear a marker labeled 1L.

Big Cypress National Preserve only recently trimmed and cleared
deadfall from the tunnel to allow paddlers to make it through to Barron
River. This is also where you begin to encounter the markers 1L though
15L. This is an intimate tunnel and lots of maneuvering is required.
Leather ferns and small mangroves line the sides. Time your trip to
catch an outgoing tide and you rocket right along through here on a
meandering west toward Barron River. If you're traveling on a lower
tide stage, the mangrove roots are stained dark from the previous high
tide and you rapidly descend below the level of the muddy bank.

You enter an opening and make a hard right to continue west/
northwest. At a little more than 3 miles from the canoe launch, the
canopy begins to break and the creek widens. You soon arrive at a pond.
Continue meandering west and you soon enter another pond from
which the creek flows southwest and then sharply northwest. Paddle
through this and you enter a large bay. This is the easternmost of the
Barron River lakes, just over 3½ miles from the canoe launch. Stay
along the left shoreline and paddle about ¾ mile to enter the next lake.
When you arrive at this lake, which is relatively narrow where you enter
at its northern tip, turn right and begin paddling north/northeast. *Note:*
At this point you intersect the trip in this guide called Halfway Creek
to Everglades City (route 8). Turn left here and reverse the directions

for that route to reach Everglades City, about 1½ miles west.

A little more than 4½ miles from the canoe launch, you come around a bend and see a passage leading away to the left. Don't turn left. This leads to a little chain of lakes, but really nowhere else. Continue paddling straight; the creek goes around a bend and soon the canopy threatens to close over, but it opens again and widens slightly. At just over 4¾ miles, you come to a point where you have four options. You continue to paddle straight, even though it looks as if you're headed into a dead end. At the north corner you'll see a narrow passage. At a little over 5 miles into your trip, the creek constricts, turns briefly into a tunnel, and opens up again. You'll see places where boats have come through and cut the way clear. After another ¼ mile you have the option to head into a creek to the right or continue on the wider portion of this creek, headed north (there may be a marker here). Continue north along the wider creek. Soon the creek constricts considerably. At 5¾ miles from the canoe ramp, you have the option to paddle straight ahead with the wide part of the creek or make a sharp left. Paddling straight ahead leads to a dead end, so make the sharp left to continue northeast. The creek narrows and then widens dramatically into a pond, and then you curve around to the northeast about 60 degrees to continue.

At about 6 miles into the trip, follow the creek as it bends to the right and then back to the left, southeast to east. You then enter a pond where it looks as if there are four directions you can go. Head to the right, where the creek looks as if it might become a tunnel, but does not. Follow the creek as it flows east and then south and then back east before bending back to the southeast. You'll pass beautiful buttonwoods with airplants nestled among the branches. As the creek narrows you pass a few cabbage palms growing close to the water's edge, one much taller than the others. The canopy closes briefly over the creek and opens again.

After a few hundred feet more, you come upon a cabbage palm fallen halfway across the creek, but bent so that its top is upright again. The ferns nestled in the cabbage palm boots are serpent ferns. Paddle a few hundred feet more to enter a small bay, with cabbage palms all

> In about two hours we entered the mouth of a creek near the head of an
> unnamed bay....No less than six lakes, each concealed from the rest by
> dense growth of littoral forest, were crossed before we reached our desti-
> nation....I cannot understand how anyone first could have found his way
> through this labyrinth or, once accomplished, ever follow it again.
> —Charles Torrey Simpson, *In Lower Florida Wilds*

around. The path to the northeast leads to a couple shallow, lovely
ponds with mangroves and saw grass crowding their edges. Continue
east to cross the bay, skirting either side of the island at its southeast
corner. If you stay to the left shore of the bay, you pass a tiny island near
the bank with a cabbage palm and snags covered with airplants. Paddle
through a very short creek at the southeast end of the bay and intersect
Halfway Creek at marker 3. Turn left to paddle north up Halfway Creek.
Bear to the right at marker 2. As you come around marker 1, you'll see
Seagrape Canal in front of you on the other side of the pond at the top
of Halfway Creek. Paddle up Seagrape Canal about 1 mile to return to
the canoe ramp.

10. *Marshlands and Halfway Creek Headwaters*

> **Trip highlights:** Scenic marshes, headwaters of Halfway Creek
> **Charts/maps:** Waterproof Chart #40E
> **Trip rating:** Easy
> **Estimated total time:** 2–3 hours
> **Total distance:** About 3 nautical miles round trip
> **Hazards:** Possible shallow water and mud on old airboat trails
> **Launch site:** Seagrape Drive
> **Ownership:** Big Cypress National Preserve (239-695-4111)
> **Alternate routes:** Lengthen round trip by 3 miles to include intro-
> duction to mangrove tunnels by paddling down Halfway Creek
> and turning around at marker 7.

General Information
This is a short paddle that provides a nice introduction to some of the
major southwest Florida habitats you'll see on longer tours through the

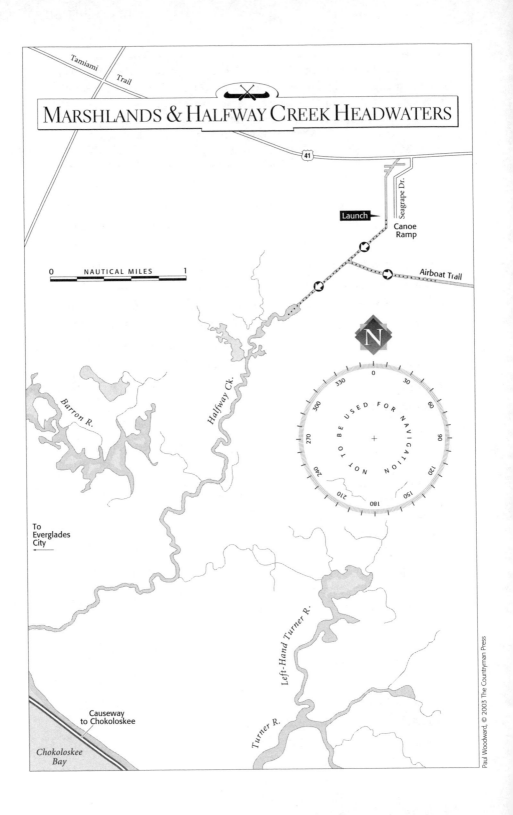

MARSHLANDS & HALFWAY CREEK HEADWATERS

Tamiami Trail

41

Seagrape Dr.

Launch

Canoe Ramp

Airboat Trail

0   NAUTICAL MILES   1

N

NOT TO BE USED FOR NAVIGATION

0   30   60   90   120   150   180   210   240   270   300   330

Barron R.

Halfway Ck.

To Everglades City

Left-Hand Turner R.

Turner R.

Causeway to Chokoloskee

Chokoloskee Bay

Big Cypress Swamp and 10,000 Islands. It begins at the Seagrape Drive canoe ramp and follows the canal a short distance to an old airboat trail, which leads you through a wonderful marsh with clear water, wide-open sky, and classic marsh dotted by little tree islands. The birding is good, offering possible views of black-necked stilts, various duck species, swallow-tailed kites, and an assortment of wading birds.

The route takes the airboat trail back to Seagrape Canal and then continues south on the canal to the headwaters of Halfway Creek before returning via Seagrape Canal to the canoe ramp. The alternate route adds 3 miles round trip and introduces you to more of Halfway Creek and its mangrove tunnels. There is no shade on this route unless you paddle down to the mangrove tunnel, so consider bringing an umbrella or two, particularly if it's hot and you have small children with you.

Access
Travel east on US 41 (Tamiami Trail) about 2½ miles from the inter-

A family paddles the scenic marshes that surround Seagrape Canal

section of US 41 and FL 29. Turn right on Seagrape Drive, just before you reach Big Cypress National Preserve headquarters. Follow Seagrape Drive about ½ mile until it dead-ends at the canoe launch.

Route

Paddle south down Seagrape Canal from the canoe ramp about ⅓ mile to the white PVC markers indicating the old airboat trail on the left. Turn left and follow the trail about ½ mile east. The airboat trail is indicated by a dotted line on your Waterproof Chart #40E. The water is shallow and crystal clear. You should easily see various types of fish and even crayfish along the edges of the trail. The surrounding marsh is comprised mainly of panic grass, cordgrass, and some saw grass, as well as areas of cattails. Small mangroves and tree islands dot the marsh. It's beautiful in late afternoon light, especially if you want to check out the reflections of big clouds billowing over the mangrove forests to the south.

At the ½-mile mark you come to a wide, shallow pond that easily allows you to turn your boat around and paddle back to Seagrape Canal. When you reach the canal, turn left and continue paddling south another ⅔ mile to a lake, the headwaters of Halfway Creek. The lake is bordered by mangroves, buttonwoods, and tall cabbage palms. Paddle around the lake close to the shoreline to look at all the airplants and even a few orchids. Small songbirds warble from the dense, shady mangrove interior.

To return, head 1 mile north on the canal to the canoe ramp. If you want to extend your trip to see more of Halfway Creek and a little bit of the mangrove tunnels, continue paddling southwest down Halfway Creek, following the white numbered markers 1–6. Just past marker 6 you enter the mangrove tunnel. Paddle through the tunnel to marker 7, where it is wide enough to turn around and paddle north about 2¾ miles to the canoe ramp. See the directions for route 8 or 9 for an expanded description of Halfway Creek and the route between the canoe ramp and marker 7.

Gradually as we ascend the stream it finally loses its character and becomes a mere, ill-defined, shallow drain for the swamp from which it flows. The Everglades lie just before us stretching away in monotonous grandeur; saw grass and other low vegetation cover the soft mud; the channel is finally lost in a network of slight depressions and the stream becomes merged into the mighty prairie. —Charles Torrey Simpson, *In Lower Florida Wilds*

11. *Turner River South from US 41*

Trip highlights: Diverse habitat, mangrove tunnels
Charts/maps: Waterproof Chart #40E, park map
Trip rating: Easy to Moderate
Estimated total time: 5–6 hours
Total distance: About 7½ nautical miles one way
Hazards: Hydrilla during low water, motorboats, possible strong winds and tide on the lower Turner River
Launch site: Adjacent US 41 Bridge over Turner River
Ownership: Big Cypress National Preserve (239-695-4111), Everglades National Park (239-695-3311)
Alternate routes: Several opportunities along this river route to turn around for shorter day trips or a round trip back to US 41

General Information

The Turner River is named for Captain Richard Turner, because of the home that he built along its banks. Turner was a guide for the ill-fated Parkhill expedition during the Third Seminole War. In late November 1857, Captain John Parkhill led 75 men up what was then called Chokolisca Creek on an expedition to find Seminoles and destroy their villages. The expedition paddled up the river for 9 miles and then hiked into the swamp toward higher ground. On the fourth day Captain Parkhill and five of his men were killed in an ambush while crossing a stream, ending the expedition. He was then buried at the forks of the Fakahatchee River.

There are two routes to paddle on the Turner River. One very short route takes you north of US 41 to the cypress-lined headwaters of the

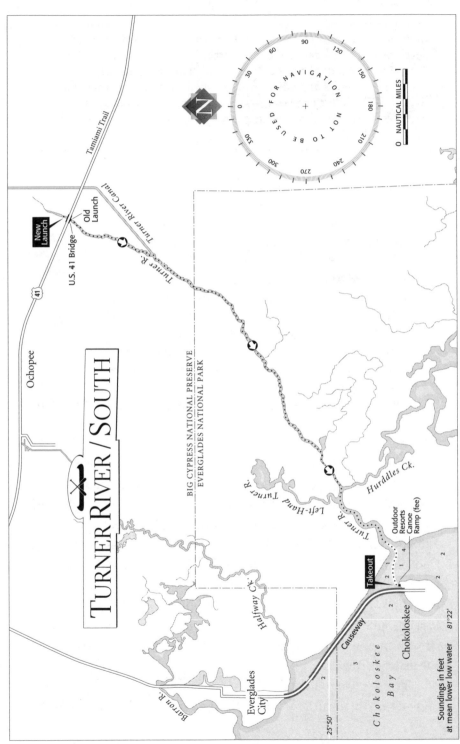

TURNER RIVER / SOUTH

Tamiami Trail

Ochopee

41

U.S. 41 Bridge

New Launch

Old Launch

Turner River Canal

Turner R.

BIG CYPRESS NATIONAL PRESERVE
EVERGLADES NATIONAL PARK

Left-Hand Turner R.

Turner R.

Hurddles Ck.

Outdoor Resorts
Canoe Ramp (fee)

1   4

2

2

2

Takeout

Halfway Ck.

Everglades City

Barron R.

Causeway

2

3

2

2

Chokoloskee

Chokoloskee Bay

81°22'

25°50'

Soundings in feet
at mean lower low water

NOT TO BE USED FOR NAVIGATION

N

30 60 90 120 150 180 210 240 270 300 330 0

0   NAUTICAL MILES   1

Paul Woodward, © 2003 The Countryman Press

Turner River. This longer route leads you south from US 41 through the Turner River's famous mangrove tunnels to Everglades City. Many people like to create their own route by paddling a combination of the two.

The Turner River Canoe Trail is arguably the most popular river route for day paddlers in the 10,000 Islands. It's a straightforward, well-groomed route with few opportunities to get lost, and there are several lakes in which to turn around so you can create a trip of virtually any length. Wildlife abounds, including alligators, turtles, vast numbers of robins in January and other songbirds throughout the year, virtually all of the species of wading birds found in the region, ospreys, various butterflies, otter, and even deer. The scenery is beautiful and varied.

You start your tour beside giant cypress trees, maples, pond apples dripping with airplants, and willows that shoulder against embankments of cutgrass and saw grass before suddenly giving way to a series of mangrove tunnels and open areas of marsh. When the tunnels end you find yourself paddling the classic 10,000 Islands landscape of mangrove-lined waterways interspersed with wide lakes that characterize the lower half of the river as it winds toward Chokoloskee. Turner River Canoe Trail briefly intersects Hurddles Creek as it nears Chokoloskee before breaking off to the southwest and passing a large complex of Calusa shell mounds near its mouth.

Kayaks are popular and efficient for traveling this route, although you should use a boat shorter than 16 feet and bring either a paddle that breaks down or a short canoe paddle for the tunnels. Canoes work fine as well, although when the water is high, you spend a lot of time ducking in the tunnels, and a big aluminum boat can bottom out when water levels are low. If you plan to paddle all the way to Chokoloskee, leave a car at Outdoor Resorts (there is a ramp fee) or the causeway on Chokoloskee, or arrange a shuttle back to your vehicle from a local outfitter. *Note:* Use extreme caution when unloading your boats and gear. Traffic along US 41 whizzes by at 60 miles per hour or more. Stay well off the road.

Access
From Everglades City, travel north on FL 29 to US 41. Turn right and

head east on southbound US 41 for 6 miles to the gravel canoe launch on the southeast corner of the bridge over Turner River. Big Cypress National Preserve is constructing a new canoe launch and small parking area on the northwest side of the bridge that will be completed by summer 2004.

Route
Before you paddle, pick up the map and description of Everglades National Park's Gulf Coast Area Canoe Trips from either Big Cypress National Preserve or the Gulf Coast Ranger Station in Everglades City. It offers a nice depiction of the Turner River Canoe Trail to supplement your Waterproof Chart #40E.

Begin your trip by heading south from the canoe ramp. The river here is narrow, shallow, clear, and unfortunately choked with hydrilla. Paddling isn't difficult when there is enough water, but in March or April the water level can be low, and hydrilla, an exotic aquatic weed escaped from the aquarium trade, forms a dense salad almost impossible to move through. Willow, cypress, maple, and sable palms line the riverbank. You quickly arrive at a small pond often brimming with little alligators. In fact, you may see more alligators in the upper 2 miles of this river than you will paddling anywhere else in the region. Night herons sometimes nest in the trees on the west edge of the pond. The river narrows after the pond and begins a series of gradual curves, with cutgrass, saw grass, and trees common to south Florida freshwater swamps crowding from the sides. Giant leather ferns appear after about ⅓ mile, and about ½ mile down you come upon beautiful water lilies on the right.

Just beyond the water lilies, you encounter the first of the red mangroves, and soon after, the first mangrove tunnel. A tunnel in sunshine is often a riot of color—emerald leaves and a blue sky reflecting on the reddish current flowing beneath. Decaying mangrove leaves lie like orange-and-red jewels on the river bottom dappled in sunlight. When a cloud passes over, the colors in the tunnel quiet and shift toward a uniform, luminous green.

You pass by more water lilies as the tunnel briefly opens and then

Alligators

The only alligator in North America is the American alligator *(Alligator mississippiensis)*. The name *alligator* comes from the Spanish word *el lagarto,* meaning "the lizard". Most routes in this guide do not take you through areas regularly frequented by alligators, with the exception of the upper freshwater reaches of rivers such as Turner River, East River, Faka Union River, and Halfway Creek. Alligators can tolerate brackish water, but they prefer it sweeter. Despite the fact that you may not see an alligator on every trip (some people are glad of this), the impact of the alligator is felt throughout the freshwater Everglades and Big Cypress Swamp.

One moniker given the gator is Architect of the Everglades, and while this may seem a bit much to people acquainted with how the south Florida landscape is shaped by changes in sea level, seed distribution, weather patterns, basic geologic processes, and the hand of humans, alligators definitely have their snouts in the design for plumbing. Where there are alligators, particularly in marshes, prairies, and cypress strands,

A baby alligator dozes in the sun on a dead palm overhanging the Turner River

you often have alligator holes. Alligators excavate holes with their snout and tail that may span nearly 40 feet in diameter and several feet deep; these holes are in mud and soft soil near a water source. Alligators may also modify existing shallow ponds, such as those in the center of a cypress strand, enlarging and deepening them. Within the hole will be one or several caverns or burrows that the alligator uses for shelter. Alligator trails from the holes may help flood surrounding marsh areas at the onset of the rainy season.

An alligator hole may be virtually invisible during the rainy season because water covers the landscape; you may notice only an abrupt difference in vegetation bordering the hole from that of the surrounding area. During the dry season, though, as surrounding water pools and then disappears altogether, the alligator hole generally retains water and becomes an oasis for virtually every living thing for miles around, including various insects, fish, frogs, turtles, wading birds, bobcats, and otters. Of course, the alligator periodically exacts rent by consuming one of the other residents in the hole, as do the residents consume each other, but the benefits the hole provides to wildlife definitely outweigh the risks of living in such a close community.

Alligator nest-building also provides a service to wildlife and the landscape beyond its primary purpose as an incubator for baby gators. Florida red-bellied turtles often excavate holes in an active alligator nest to allow the heat (generated by the sun and decaying vegetation that comprises the nest) to incubate their eggs and take advantage of the female gator to unwittingly guard turtle eggs in addition to her own. An alligator nest may contain up to 200 turtle eggs from several different individuals. The peat created by the construction and ultimate decay of the alligator nest provides critical nutrients to surrounding plant life.

Alligators can grow to be quite large, but never as large as people think they are. Males max out at about 14 feet long, while females reach only 10 feet or so. They are generally black to olive brown in color on top, with white bellies and greenish eyes. Young alligators are black with yellow stripes on the tail, which they lose as they grow older. Unlike crocodiles, whose teeth protrude from both the upper and lower jaw, alligator teeth protrude only from the upper jaw because the lower set of teeth fit into depressions in the upper jaw. Although an alligator's snout is typically broader than a crocodile's, and its color generally darker, looking at the tooth pattern when the jaws are closed is the best way to tell them apart, particularly in brackish areas where alligators and crocodiles both may be found.

Alligators can't maintain a constant internal temperature as we do, and therefore, their body temperature fluctuates with their surroundings. Alligators often warm themselves up by crawling out of the water to sun on a log or muddy bank. If they become too warm, they crawl back into the water, or they crawl partially into the water and leave a portion of their body exposed, thereby maintaining a comfortable temperature without having to shift again for most of the day. Although they seem ponderous and sluggish on land, they can move with astonishing speed and are capable of outrunning a person over a short distance. In the water, they swim with their legs folded at their sides, sweeping their tail from side to side for propulsion.

Alligators are opportunistic and will eat almost anything they perceive as potentially tasty. Hatchling gators eat apple snails, insects, crayfish, tiny fish, and frogs, while larger alligators often feast on turtles, fish, birds, snakes, small mammals, and even other alligators. Its normal diet does not include people, but an alligator may become aggressive if it perceives people as providers of food. Once fed by humans, the gator does not forget it. This practice is dangerous not only to people but to the gator as well, for an aggressive animal will eventually be deemed a nuisance and destroyed.

Both male and female alligators bellow during the mating season, and individuals can recognize one another from their bellows. The literature generally states that courtship commences at the onset of the rainy season in May and females begin constructing nests in June and July. However, I have heard hearty bellowing in February and seen pods of 8-inch-long baby gators swimming along the edges of the Turner River in January. Perhaps that is the nature of the south Florida wilderness, where water level drives most everything.

A female alligator lays some 40 leathery eggs that are incubated for several weeks in a mound of rotting vegetation that she has scraped together. The sex of the babies is determined by the temperature of the eggs during the first three weeks. The hot sun typically raises the temperature near the top of the nest, so the embryos in those eggs become males, while the eggs in the relatively cooler bottom of the nest yield females. When the baby gators are ready to emerge from the eggs, they begin chipping away at the shell with a special egg tooth at the tip of the snout, emitting a little hiccupping sound. This prompts the mother to tear away the top of the nest, flipping the babies into the water as she tears into the nest with her front legs. She may also take eggs gently into her mouth and crack them to help release the babies inside. The mother gator may watch over her brood for as little as a few days to as long as several months.

closes in again. The mangroves here are primarily red mangroves—small, dense, with interlocking arching spidery roots. Many drip with giant catopsis and other airplants. The river bottom is for the most part hard-packed sand. When you emerge from the tunnel into a nice pond, keep to the right to pick up the next tunnel. If you have been paddling at a steady pace, you are probably a half hour from the canoe launch.

The roof of this second tunnel drops even lower than the first, and you may need to do the limbo to make your way through. This tunnel is somewhat longer than the first. If you are using a kayak with a rudder, drop the rudder because it will otherwise catch overhanging limbs and roots, sending you careening into the trees. A couple of wide spots in this tunnel offer clearings that allow you to get out and stretch your legs, or if you wish, turn your boat around and paddle back to the canoe launch. If you are paddling quietly alone through the tunnel near dusk, you may see deer in the mangroves along the edge. Kingfishers most certainly will scold as they race in front of you down the tunnel.

After paddling just under 1 mile, you reach a wide spot in the mangroves where the tunnel disappears for about 20 feet and freshwater swamp encroaches on your left. There are a few mangroves mixed in, plus a cabbage palm, leather fern, swamp lily, and purple pickerel weed. These plants indicate that despite the mangroves, you are still in relatively fresh water. Soon you will arrive at another beautiful pond, also choked unfortunately with hydrilla. You may see plenty of wading birds winging their way over the surrounding cordgrass marsh, where willows line the bank. This is a place to get out if you need to.

The river soon splits, and you can go either way and wind up back at the main channel. You begin to see more swamp lilies, custard apple trees, Brazilian pepper, and cattails, plus mangroves and wide prairie. You'll probably see scars from old airboat trails. The river is fairly wide and broadens into shallow lakes.

You encounter another short mangrove tunnel after paddling just over 1½ miles from the canoe launch and then pop out into the open with marsh on the left and mangroves on the right. At just over 1¾ miles, you continue southwest through another mangrove tunnel, passing a sign indicating the boundary of Everglades National Park.

After paddling about 2¼ miles from the launch site, the river opens up a little, the water is beautiful and clear, and occasional large buttonwoods draped in airplants grace the shoreline. The water is about 4 feet deep here and the river bottom is firm sand.

Soon you arrive at a small pond with a cut in the mangroves to the right that leads to a nice place to get out and stretch your legs. This is also a good place to turn around if you intend on paddling only a leisurely half-day trip. Continue down the pond into a short tunnel. When you come out of this tunnel, you may hear a small creek on your left trickling down through the mangroves. Continue southwest down the main part of the channel through a stretch of wider water that leads to another long, quiet, lovely tunnel. Look for fish in the clear water at the edge of the mangroves.

By 3 miles from the canoe launch, you have left the tunnels for good and will paddle along a narrow stretch of river lined by mangroves and tall cabbage palms. The Turner remains quiet, somewhat narrow, and very beautiful for another 1¼ miles. At 4¼ miles the river becomes more noticeably tidal and no freshwater vegetation remains. At just under 5 miles, you pass another small, canopied creek on the left. You'll soon pass a lake off to the east. Stay to the right to continue on the river paddling west/southwest.

At 5¾ miles from the canoe launch, you reach the confluence of Turner River and Hurddles Creek. Stay to the right and continue paddling west to stay on the Turner River Canoe Trail. Turner River from its confluence with Hurddles Creek onward to the mouth at Chokoloskee Bay is very wide. Watch out for motorboats from this point on. If you are lucky or have timed your trip well, you can ride the outgoing tide to Chokoloskee.

At just under 6 miles, you pass Left-Hand Turner River on your right. Stay to the left to continue west on Turner River. Also look for manatees in this wide part of the river, particularly at the confluence with Left-Hand Turner. At 6¼ miles you pass a water monitoring station on the right side of the river. A Calusa shell mound occupies the left bank of the river just beyond the next to last bend in the river, which is about ¾ mile from the river mouth. Watch out for oyster bars

> You rarely find one [a frog] hunting in the daytime, and even more rarely in a mangrove tree. But this one was in a perfect frenzy of mosquito-catching. It was a drizzly day and there were so many mosquitoes it was hard to breathe, yet I noticed that not one of them sat on the naked frog. It seemed totally immune to the hordes, as if shielded from them by some personal secretion of bug repellent. —Archie Carr, *The Everglades*

from this point on to the mouth of the river, which is indicated by a channel marker. Chokoloskee is visible from the river mouth, and you can easily set a course for Outdoor Resorts boat ramp, the causeway, or wherever your take-out point on the island may be. Paddle ½ mile from the mouth of Turner River to reach Chokoloskee.

12. *Turner River North from US 41*

Trip highlights: Beautiful cypress and freshwater swamp, abundant wildlife

Charts/maps: Waterproof Chart #40E

Trip rating: Easy

Estimated total time: 1–2 hours

Total distance: About 1 nautical mile round trip

Hazards: Possibly choked with hydrilla during late spring and low water

Launch site: Adjacent US 41 Bridge over Turner River

Ownership: Big Cypress National Preserve (239-695-4111)

Alternate routes: Combine with Turner River Canoe Trail paddling south from US 41 through first mangrove tunnel to lengthen the round trip to 2½ miles.

General Information

This is a short, scenic, very easy paddle from the canoe ramp at US 41 north to the headwaters of Turner River. For more information about the Turner River, see the Turner River South from US 41 Trail (route 11).

Expect to see alligators, wading birds, anhingas, kingfishers, an osprey nest perched in the crown of a giant bald cypress, and lots of fish. This route is confined to fresh water, and like the beginning of the

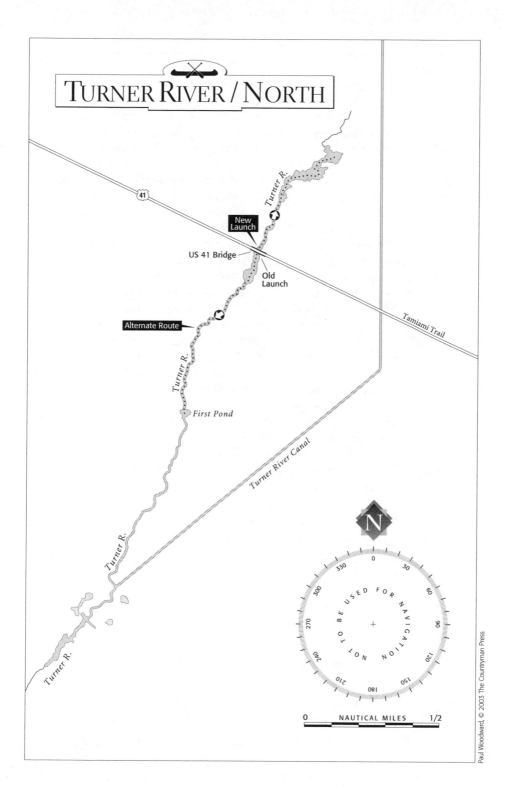

TURNER RIVER / NORTH

41

Turner R.

New Launch

US 41 Bridge

Old Launch

Alternate Route

Turner R.

First Pond

Turner R.

Turner River Canal

Tamiami Trail

Turner R.

N

NOT TO BE USED FOR NAVIGATION

0   30   60   90   120   150   180   210   240   270   300   330

0   NAUTICAL MILES   1/2

Paul Woodward, © 2003 The Countryman Press

Cypress

If you drive along the Tamiami Trail or paddle the Turner River in the Big Cypress Swamp in December or January, you'll notice vast areas of trees with no leaves. Most of these trees are cypress, and they are not dead, despite that perception by many visitors as they view the leafless landscape while reveling in the balmy 80+ -degree temperature. Although cypress are conifers in the family *Taxodiaceae* and so are related to redwoods, they are among only four cone-bearing trees that are deciduous, meaning they drop their needles in late fall. The others include the American larch, the European larch, and the dawn redwood from China. The bald cypress is so named because it is bald during winter.

Bald cypress and pond cypress, once considered by some botanists to be separate species, are now widely considered varieties of the same species, *Taxodium distichum,* in part because they freely interbreed in many places. Bald cypress grows best in areas of deeper, moving water; while pond cypress can grow in areas of shallow, stagnant water with a long dry-down. Pond cypress can grow in areas with very little soil and nutrients, often becoming stunted and twisted. These are often called dwarf cypress, scrub cypress, or hat-rack cypress. Bald cypress is reputed to be the largest tree growing in North America east of the Rocky Mountains. One can grow to more than 150 feet tall and 6 feet in diameter. Both varieties can live for several hundred years.

Cypress trees are either male or female and can be sexed by their flowers. The male flowers are small and purple and hang in drupes, somewhat like grapes from last year's new twigs. Female flowers are very small and once fertilized become cones that contain about 30 seeds. Cy-

Turner River Canoe Trail, can be choked with hydrilla, an exotic aquatic weed escaped from the aquarium trade. Hydrilla is at its worst when water level drops in late spring. This route offers the best paddling opportunity to see bald cypress trees in the Big Cypress Swamp. It is an ideal dawn or late afternoon paddle.

Access

From Everglades City, travel north on FL 29 to US 41. Turn right and head east on southbound US 41 for 6 miles to the gravel canoe launch on the southeast corner of the bridge over Turner River. Big Cypress National Preserve is constructing a new canoe launch and small parking area on the northwest side of the bridge that will be completed by

press seeds are primarily dispersed by water, although a few animals, such as wood ducks and at one time the now extinct Carolina parakeet, do eat and disperse them. Cypress seeds can't germinate underwater, and cypress seedlings can't be flooded above their needles or they will die, primary reasons why the yearly dry-downs in swamps or periodic changes in river water level are critical to the recruitment of new cypress trees.

One unusual characteristic of both pond and bald cypress is the cypress *knee.* The precise function of these knees, which are vertical extensions of the root system, is still argued, but the prevailing theories state that they help aerate the tree's root system and may provide additional stability in the muck in which the trees typically grow. No cypress knee is exactly the same as another, and they often resemble gnomes. Cypress knees on larger trees can grow to 12 feet high.

Bald cypress is found throughout the South from Delaware through Florida and west into Texas, north into southern Illinois and Indiana. It has been planted successfully as far north as Chicago. Pond cypress extends north as far as Virginia. Virtually all of the old-growth trees more than 600 years old have been cut in the South, although small old-growth stands still exist at the Big Cypress Bend Boardwalk in Fakahatchee Strand and at National Audubon Society's Corkscrew Swamp Sanctuary northeast of Naples. Cypress is still harvested to some degree for sawtimber and on a much larger scale for mulch. Most conservation-minded individuals refuse to buy cypress mulch because of the continued threat to swamps cypress logging presents.

summer 2004. *Note:* Use extreme caution when unloading your boats and gear at the side of the road. Traffic along US 41 whizzes by at 60 miles per hour or more. Stay well off the road.

Route

Begin by paddling north from the canoe ramp. This may be easier said than done if the river is low. Mats of hydrilla will be floating at the surface. Even the little alligators have a hard time swimming through the stuff. The river is narrow and winds gently, bounded on the shore by bald cypress, maples, oaks, willows, cattails, cabbage palms, swamp dogwood, pond apples, and various vines. After about 2/10 mile you begin to see large cypress trees, some of them virgin trees that may be as

A kayak tour paddling the north section of the Turner River

much as 600 years old. All around you will hear a riot of birdsong that becomes more apparent as you distance yourself from the highway noise of US 41. Listen for barred owls, Carolina wrens, Northern parula warblers, blue-gray gnatcatchers, and belted kingfishers. Some you may see, others will be high in the crowns of trees. This is a good area to look for common moorhens and green herons. Gar may startle you when they thrash at the water's surface.

On the left after about ¼ mile, you will see a tall bald cypress with an osprey nest in the crown. In winter and spring, the ospreys will probably be in the nest with eggs or chicks.

Just beyond the osprey nest, the river widens into a large lake ringed with old stumps, willows, cattails, and more large cypress. There are also small islands. It's a tranquil place. Amazing damselflies, diminutive relatives of dragonflies, flit around your boat like lightbulb filaments given wings. A red-shouldered hawk cries from somewhere in the cypress forest. In March or April you may see swallow-tailed kites

> Sometimes the stream flows through a cypress swamp and in it will be found much of interest.... The great trunks have conical, fluted, or buttressed bases, and in large specimens may be eighteen feet or more in diameter at the ground.... Scattered through the swamp are erect, conical, woody growths known as "cypress knees," sometimes as tall as a man or even more, with neither branches nor leaves. To one who has never seen them before they are certainly most incomprehensible.
> —Charles Torrey Simpson, *In Lower Florida Wilds*

skimming the lake surface for a drink. Take time to explore the edge of the lake to look for frogs, bitterns, or other shy creatures. You will probably see alligators in the lake as well.

After you have explored the lake, head south downriver back to the canoe launch. You can easily extend this trip by another 1½ miles by paddling south under US 41. Continue through the first mangrove tunnel before turning around in the small pond at the end of the tunnel and returning to the canoe ramp.

Tall bald cypress

PART V
Everglades City

*E*verglades City proclaims itself as the Gateway to the 10,000 Islands, and for paddlers that is most certainly true. It is one end of the Wilderness Waterway, the famous Everglades backcountry route linking Everglades City to Flamingo. It is the best place in the 10,000 Islands to rent canoes or kayaks, hook up with a guided paddling excursion, or find a comfortable room from which to base your explorations of Big Cypress National Preserve, Everglades National Park, and Fakahatchee Strand State Preserve. It even has a tiny airport, so you can fly in or book a float plane tour to get a bird's-eye view of the islands before putting your paddle to the water.

Prior to 1923, Everglades City was called Everglade, a name given the settlement along the crooked little Allen's River in 1893 by Bembery Storter after the U.S. Post Office refused the request for the name Chokoloskee. Farming was the primary occupation of people living in the area and included sugarcane, bananas, and vegetables. Allen gave Everglades City its start, but George T. Storter is considered the true founder of the town. He and his family were prominent in Everglade's growth and activities and owned much of the land around the town until the arrival of Barron Collier in 1923. It was under the Storter stewardship that Everglade began to draw winter visitors and sportsmen. The Rod and Gun Club was built around the old Storter home.

Barron Collier is primarily responsible for the foundation of Everglades City as you see it today. In 1923 he and his company purchased most of the land in and surrounding the town. Within five years the sleepy trading post and farming community was converted into a bustling industrial-based company town replete with roads, a railroad, a bank, a telephone, sawmills, a boatyard, churches, a school, workers' barracks and mess halls, and even its own streetcar at one time. The Ivey House, home of NACT-Everglades Rentals and Eco Adventures, was once one of the Collier Company workers' barracks.

With the establishment of Everglades National Park and subsequent purchase of most of Big Cypress Swamp and the 10,000 Islands for conservation, Everglades City once again looks to the natural environment for economic viability through nature tourism, sportfishing, and commercial crabbing. Everglades National Park was formally dedicated in Everglades City on December 6, 1947. The Gulf Coast Visitor Center of Everglades National Park is perched at the edge of the Chokoloskee Bay, and many of the paddling routes in this section depart from the canoe ramp behind the maintenance buildings.

More so than with any other routes in this guide, pay attention to tide times for routes originating from Everglades City. The tidal range is less than 5 feet, but it seems as if all the water in the western Everglades wants to either rush in or rush out of Sandfly and Indian Key Passes, in particular, in the shortest possible time. For paddle trips to the islands, leave on an outgoing tide and return on an incoming tide. For paddle trips into the interior, such as those on the Barron River, follow the incoming tide inland or ride back to Everglades City on an outgoing tide. Try to avoid the Everglades National Park canoe ramp at dead low tide because it can be a mud hole.

Other than the canoe ramp at the national park, the only public boat ramp from which to launch is at the Barron River Marina. The Ivey House and NACT-Everglades Rentals and Eco Adventures have a canoe dock you can use if you are renting one of their boats or using their shuttle service.

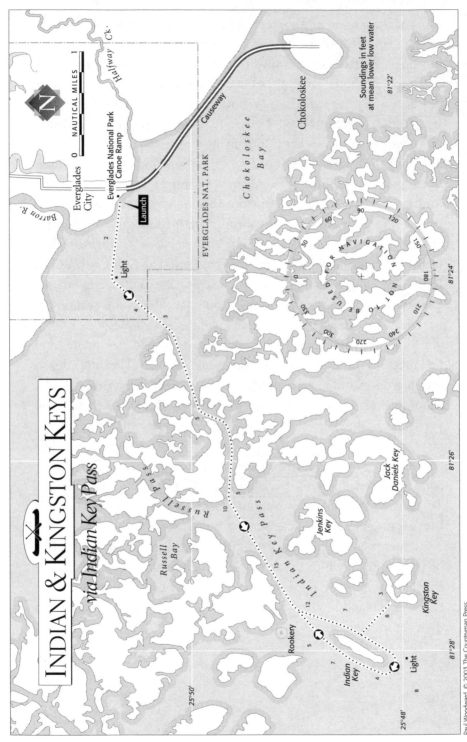

INDIAN & KINGSTON KEYS
via Indian Key Pass

N

NAUTICAL MILES

Everglades City

Barron R.

Halfway Ck.

Everglades National Park
Canoe Ramp

Launch

EVERGLADES NAT. PARK

Causeway

Chokoloskee Bay

Chokoloskee

Soundings in feet
at mean lower low water

USED FOR NAVIGATION

Light

Russell Pass

Russell Bay

Rookery

Indian Key

Light

Kingston Key

Indian Key Pass

Jenkins Key

Jack Daniels Key

81°22'
81°24'
81°26'
81°28'

25°50'
25°48'

13. *Indian and Kingston Keys via Indian Key Pass*

Trip highlights: Bird rookery, sandy beaches, interesting shoreline and sandbars
Charts/maps: Waterproof Chart #40E, NOAA Nautical Chart #11430
Trip rating: Easy
Estimated total time: 9 hours
Total distance: 12 nautical miles round trip
Hazards: Muddy launch at low tide, possible strong wind and tide, powerboats and commercial fishing boats in Indian Key Pass
Launch site: Everglades National Park canoe ramp
Ownership: Everglades National Park (239-695-3311)
Alternate routes: Paddle Indian Key Pass to Indian Key. Paddle northwest and then north 1½ miles around Stop Keys from south end of Indian Key to reach the beach at Picnic Key.

General Information

This is an easy route to navigate and the quickest trip to the outer islands within Everglades National Park. There is every type of boat to contend with, including the Everglades National Park tour boats, big commercial crab boats, fishing guide skiffs, sailboats, and recreational powerboats; but if you stay to the edge of the channel, you'll be fine. Do not linger in the marked channels.

Indian Key is a beautiful island with a wrecked mangrove shoreline to explore and a sand spit on its north end. Kingston Key also has a sandy area to visit and beautiful beach berm habitat. Preferably leave at the high stage of an outgoing tide to eliminate mud at the boat ramp and to use the tide to your advantage. Return on the incoming tide. Allow two hours time difference between the mouth of Indian Key Pass and Everglades City.

Access

From US 41 (Tamiami Trail) follow FL 29 for 3 miles south to Everglades City. Continue through town, past the traffic circle, following signs for Everglades National Park and Chokoloskee. Turn right into

Kingston Key

Everglades National Park. The canoe launch is behind the headquarters and canoe rental.

Route

Leave the Everglades National Park canoe ramp and paddle west across Chokoloskee Bay to Indian Key Pass. Ignore the channel markers near the park ramp; they connect Barron River with Sandfly Pass. Instead, look for the channel markers to the far west and powerboats entering and exiting the Barron River. You'll intersect Indian Key Pass at marker 24, where a sign welcomes you to Everglades National Park, after paddling just over 1 mile from the ranger station. Chokoloskee Bay can be too shallow to cut across at low tide, so you might need to resort to following the marked boat channel around to the mouth of the Barron River and then catching the marked channel to Indian Key Pass from there.

Continue following Indian Key Pass west through a maze of islands and oyster bars. On a cool morning at low tide, you may pass vultures loafing on mud banks and oyster bars, spreading their wings and catching a little sun. You'll paddle past bays extending from both sides of the pass. At marker 15, about 2 miles from the canoe ramp, Indian Key Pass turns southwest and then shortly reverts west, widening considerably. Paddle another 1¼ miles to reach the Gulf of Mexico.

From where you enter the Gulf, Russell Pass and Russell Bay extend away to the northwest. Watch for dolphins in this area. Adjust your course to the southwest to remain in the pass; and continue another 1¾ miles, passing the Indian Key light, to marker 4. Channel marker 4 lies between Indian and Kingston Keys. Indian Key is to your right and Kingston Key is ½ mile to the southeast on the left. You can circumnavigate the whole shoreline of Indian Key, exploring the tidal pools and shattered mangroves, and then head to a sand spit at its north tip to rest. Or, paddle straight over to the sand beach on Kingston Key. You'll see the Kingston Key camping chickee and outhouse just off the shore of Kingston Key. Return to the canoe ramp by paddling Indian Key Pass a little over 5 miles from marker 4.

If you would rather visit the gorgeous beach at Picnic Key, paddle 1½ miles northwest and then north around the Stop Keys to reach Picnic Key. If tide permits, you can split the Stop Keys and save a little distance to Picnic Key.

14. *Sandfly Island*

> **Trip highlights:** Bird rookery, sandy beaches, interesting shoreline and sandbars
> **Charts/maps:** Waterproof Chart #40E
> **Trip rating:** Moderate
> **Estimated total time:** 3 hours
> **Total distance:** About 5¼ nautical miles round trip
> **Hazards:** Muddy launch at low tide, possible strong wind and tide, powerboats in Sandfly Pass
> **Launch site:** Everglades National Park canoe ramp
> **Ownership:** Everglades National Park (239-695-3311)
> **Alternate routes:** Follow Sandfly Pass to and from Sandfly Island.

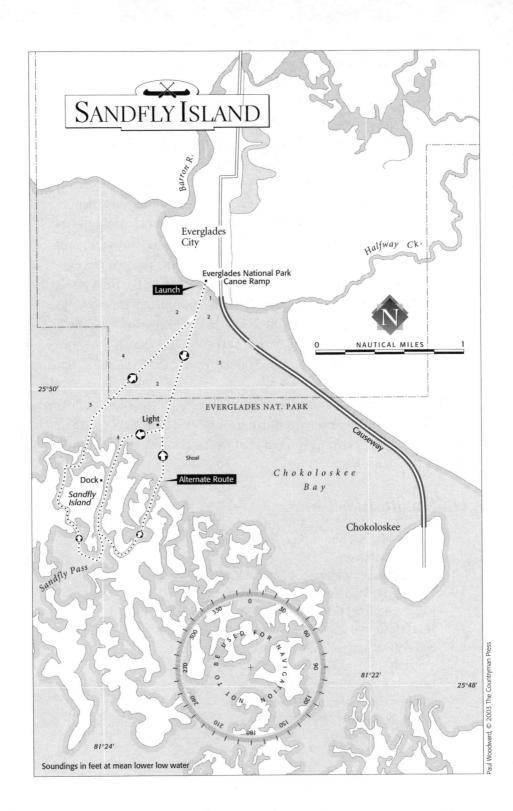

SANDFLY ISLAND

Barron R.

Everglades
City

Halfway Ck.

Everglades National Park
Canoe Ramp

Launch

1
2
2
4
3
2
4
2
3

Light

EVERGLADES NAT. PARK

Causeway

4

Shoal

Alternate Route

Chokoloskee Bay

Dock

Sandfly Island

Chokoloskee

Sandfly Pass

NOT TO BE USED FOR NAVIGATION

0
330
30
300
60
270
90
240
120
210
150
180

25°50'

81°24'

81°22'

25°48'

Soundings in feet at mean lower low water

N

0   NAUTICAL MILES   1

Paul Woodward, © 2003 The Countryman Press

General Information

The main attraction of this route is Sandfly Island and its scenic 1-mile nature trail, not the short journey getting there and back. It is an easy paddle provided the wind is not howling and you leave on an outgoing tide and return with the incoming tide. Sandfly Island has a long history of human settlement beginning with the Calusas and ending with the creation of Everglades National Park.

Settlers grew tomatoes here, and at one time, the island supported a packing shed, a store, and several homes. Barron Collier thought the island's future promising enough to drill a well there, for which he was rewarded with somewhat brackish but potable water, rare in the islands. You see ample evidence of this history as you walk past old cisterns and foundation stones, following the trail as it wanders through a mangrove forest, past an artesian well, through a grove of exotic tropical ornamental hardwoods and native trees marking an old homestead, and along a high section of trail that traverses the top of a shell mound overlooking Sandfly Pass.

Sandfly is another name for no-see-um, a tiny biting midge often referred to as jaws with wings, and the island can live up to its namesake. Pack bug repellent for your walk on the nature trail.

The paddle route follows Sandfly Pass to Sandfly Island and then circles around it. You'll follow a narrow creek along the shell mounds on the western edge of the island before returning to Chokoloskee Bay opposite your launch site from the Gulf Coast Ranger Station canoe ramp.

Access

From US 41 (Tamiami Trail) follow FL 29 for 3 miles south to Everglades City. Continue through town, around the traffic circle, following signs for Everglades National Park and Chokoloskee. Turn right into Everglades National Park. The canoe launch is behind the headquarters and canoe rental.

Route

Begin at the Everglades National Park canoe ramp. Time your trip to leave on a falling tide (preferably not at low tide to avoid the mud

A gumbo limbo reaches for the sky on Sandfly Island

around the canoe ramp) to take advantage of the tide rushing out through Sandfly Pass. Paddle south from the ramp. You pass channel markers 5 and 6, which remind boaters to watch their speed through the manatee zone. Continue south beyond channel markers 1 and 2, and turn toward the right to follow Sandfly Pass as it bends to the southwest. The channel shortly comes back around to a more southerly course, and you are able to see the outhouse at Sandfly Island, about 1½ miles from the canoe ramp. Pull your boat well up on the shell beach and then tie to a mangrove.

The Sandfly Island nature trail begins just beyond the dock. You almost immediately smell the slightly skunky odor of white stopper, a small native tropical hardwood. A boardwalk passes over a tiny creek among the mangroves. Along the trail you'll see probably the best example of tropical hardwood hammock vegetation of any of the trips in this book. The tree with the red peeling bark is gumbo limbo, also called tourist tree in honor of visitors who resemble these native hardwoods after a long day on the water without sunscreen. Wild coffee may be in bloom; look for the small shrubs with heavily veined leaves and small, pretty white flowers. Huge royal poincienna trees (which develop beautiful scarlet flowers in June) and gumbo limbos adorn the remains of a homestead. If you are quiet during your walk on the trail, you may spy a raccoon peering warily at you from behind a tree.

After you have enjoyed the nature trail, you have two choices for your return trip. The quickest and shortest way is to turn left and follow Sandfly Pass north back to Everglades City. If the tide is roaring in at this point, it is your best option.

The scenic route, detailed here, takes you right and south on Sandfly Pass, hopefully at slack tide or the beginning of the incoming tide. As you approach a sharp bend to the east/southeast, about 100 feet beyond an osprey nest on the right, turn right into an inlet and begin to paddle west/southwest. This turn is just over 2 miles from the canoe launch. You soon approach another tiny inlet and are faced with a choice of turning right or left. Turn right, tracking north. It is quiet here off the main pass and a good area to see snowy egrets, great egrets, and little blue herons. Maybe you'll see a swallow-tailed kite skimming the tops of the mangroves. The swallow-tailed kite resembles an osprey in color but has a distinctly forked tail.

The little pass continues to narrow, and as it constricts, the current increases in velocity. The pass hooks around to the northeast, and then just as it curves back toward the north/northwest, you see shell mounds rising from the edge of the water on the right side amid dead gumbo limbo trees. The current here carries you along at better than 3 knots, without any effort on your part, gurgling like a rocky brook as it passes over low branches. If you put a paddle to the water, you can do more than 6 knots. Conversely, if you catch this current on an outgoing tide, your life will be miserable as you fight for every inch of progress.

The channel swings back to the northeast at about 2½ miles from the canoe launch, and the current slows considerably. After you paddle another ½ mile, you arrive at a cut in the mangroves on your right promising (as does the chart) to lead you back to Sandfly Pass. This is a lie. Turn right, but keep to the left shoreline rather than paddling east across the small bay and entering the z-shaped creek that dead-ends with only 20 feet or so of thick mangroves and oyster bars between you and Sandfly Pass.

Paddle north through a gap in the mangroves, which is guarded by a toothy mound of oysters. Watch this at a low tide stage; and whatever you do, don't use your hands to push yourself off the bottom and through the gap. The oysters will mangle you. Paddle north across the next small bay, pass through another narrow cut in the mangroves, and reach Chokoloskee Bay. From here it's a straight northeast shot of about 1 mile across the bay back to the canoe ramp, next to the brown park buildings plainly in view.

15. *Jewell Key via Sandfly Pass*

Trip highlights: Bird rookery, sandy beaches, interesting shoreline and sandbars

Charts/maps: Waterproof Chart #40E

Trip rating: Moderate

Estimated total time: 9 hours

Total distance: 12 nautical miles round trip

Hazards: Muddy launch at low tide, possible strong wind and tide, powerboats in Sandfly Pass

Launch site: Everglades National Park canoe ramp

Ownership: Everglades National Park (239-695-3311)

Alternate routes: Leave from Chokoloskee and follow Chokoloskee Pass to Jewell Key.

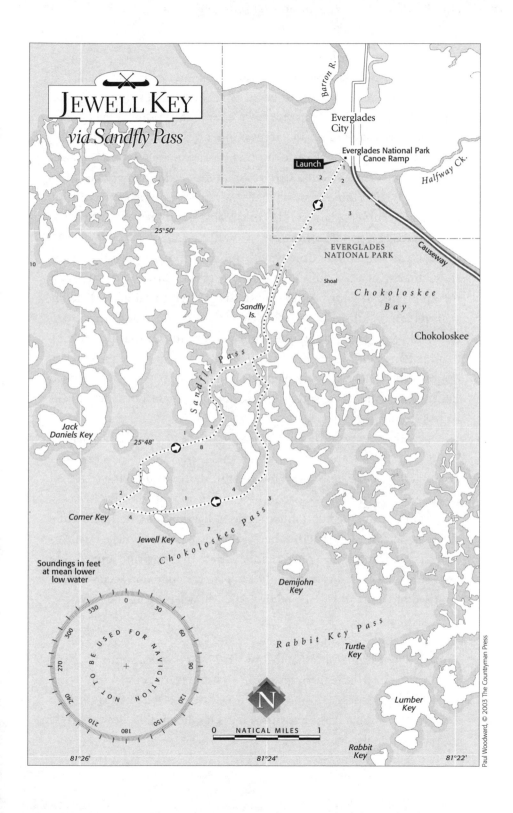

JEWELL KEY
via Sandfly Pass

Barron R.

Everglades
City

Everglades National Park
Canoe Ramp

Launch

Halfway Ck.

Causeway

25°50'

EVERGLADES
NATIONAL PARK

Shoal

*Chokoloskee
Bay*

Chokoloskee

Sandfly
Is.

Sandfly Pass

Jack
Daniels Key

25°48'

Corner Key

Jewell Key

Chokoloskee Pass

Soundings in feet
at mean lower
low water

NOT TO BE USED FOR NAVIGATION

Demijohn
Key

Rabbit Key Pass

Turtle
Key

Lumber
Key

Rabbit
Key

N

0   NATICAL MILES   1

81°26'   81°24'   81°22'

Paul Woodward, © 2003 The Countryman Press

General Information

This is a long day trip that offers beautiful scenery and the chance to see a lot of seasonal birds at either the Jewell Key rookery or the Comer Key sandbar. The route takes you from your launch point at Everglades National Park canoe ramp and across Chokoloskee Bay to Sandfly Pass. You then follow Sandfly Pass to another pass, unnamed on most charts but that appears as Vinnie's Cut on Standard Mapping Services Map #504-898-0025. Vinnie's Cut typically carries less motorboat traffic, in particular, commercial boats. This pass leads you to the Gulf of Mexico, from which you paddle southwest to Jewell Key.

You can return the same way or follow Sandfly Pass for a faster, more direct route back to the launch site, particularly if you catch the incoming tide. If your timing is off and you face an outgoing tide on your return paddle to Everglades City, take Vinnie's Cut to minimize the tidal resistance you would otherwise endure in that portion of Sandfly Pass. Once you reach Sandfly Pass, however, there is no other option but to grind your way back to Chokoloskee Bay. At Chokoloskee Bay the tidal influence is spread out, so paddling against the current will be less strenuous.

As with all trips setting out from Everglades National Park canoe ramp, time things carefully to take advantage of water at the ramp and an outgoing tide to help carry you to your destination in the outer islands. Leave the ramp as close to high tide as possible, or in the early stages of the outgoing tide. I rate the trip to Jewell Key as moderate, considering that it is a long paddle, there a couple of places to make mistakes in navigation, and you will need a lot of strength if the wind and/or tide are wrong. If you are in good condition, plan carefully, and keep yourself apprised of winds and tidal direction, the trip will probably be easy.

Access

From US 41 (Tamiami Trail) follow FL 29 for 3 miles south to Everglades City. Continue through town, past the traffic circle, following signs for Everglades National Park and Chokoloskee. Turn right into Everglades National Park. The canoe launch is behind the headquarters and canoe rental.

Route

Start from the Everglades National Park canoe launch and head almost directly due south toward Sandfly Pass. You'll see channel markers beginning in Chokoloskee Bay, and powerboats in the channel headed south will also help you identify the pass. Once you reach the channel, you'll see Sandfly Island on the right about 1½ miles from the launch site; it is marked by an outhouse on the shore. At about 2 miles Sandfly Pass bends toward the west, where there is an osprey nest on the east side. Ospreys will be on the nest with eggs or chicks from January through April.

Once you come around to the west at just over 2 miles, bear to the left to take an unmarked pass (labeled Vinnie's Cut on the map from Standard Mapping Services) south to Jewell Key. Most fishermen will tell you this cut is Sandfly Pass or that it has no name at all. To the right is a passage that leads to a beautiful wide bay and some creeks. Straight west will take you on a continuing course to Sandfly Pass. Once you enter this cut, you'll be following a southeast course of about 160 degrees.

You'll soon encounter a wide bay with a mangrove island in the middle. Stay to the right of the island and continue following the pass. You'll pass another osprey nest on the left.

Once you exit Vinnie's Cut, there is a clump of trees about 1 mile out either directly ahead or just to your right, depending on where you exit the cut. This is the Jewell Key rookery. The much larger island just to the right of the rookery is Jewell Key. You'll see a narrow cut that divides it from the neighboring island as you approach the beach. Water flows through the cut toward the Gulf of Mexico on the outgoing tide and then inland toward Sandfly Pass on the incoming tide.

Once you land on Jewell Key, there is a nice sand beach to have lunch or stretch out and relax. Watch the oyster shells on the west side of the sand spit. They are extremely sharp and can inflict nasty wounds. As the tide comes in, you may see horseshoe crabs coming to mate and lay their eggs on the sand beach. If you arrive at a lower tide stage, take time to explore the exposed rocky shoreline, as well as the island's western shoreline with its shattered mangrove crags, tidal pools, and rock bottom.

Look out from Jewell Key's sand spit at about 300 degrees to see a long, treeless, sandy island. In winter, you may not notice the sand because it is often covered completely on its northern end by white pelicans, Forster's terns, black skimmers, American oystercatchers, sanderlings, willets, and other shorebirds. This is Comer Key. Camping is no longer permitted on Comer Key because it now has a nasty habit of disappearing at high tide, although most charts still show a camping symbol and trees. Comer Key, previously named Pelican Key and before that Bird Key, was the site of the homestead of a hermit named Robert Roy Osmer. Osmer remained on the island until Hurricane Donna destroyed his shack and erased nearly every trace of vegetation from the island in 1960.

From the Jewell Key cut, paddle west about ½ mile toward Comer Key. As you approach Comer Key, keep a respectful distance from the birds. If you see them begin to shuffle and fidget, or get up and walk around, then you are too close and need to back off. Please avoid causing the birds to take flight because that forces them to burn pre-

White pelicans on Comer Key

White Pelicans

I find the white pelicans particularly interesting from mid-February though May as they develop a peculiar orange, platelike protuberance on the upper mandible. This is part of their breeding plumage. Most adult white pelicans leave the 10,000 Islands in April or May to nest on the edges of large lakes in the upper western United States. The adults' protuberance falls off once the eggs have hatched and they are feeding chicks.

White pelicans differ significantly from brown pelicans in size, color, and feeding habits. White pelicans are much larger and mostly white with black wingtips; brown pelicans are mostly brownish or grayish. White pelicans feed cooperatively in groups by encircling a school of fish in shallow water and then scooping up the prey. Brown pelicans feed individually by diving into the water to catch fish near the surface.

In both species of pelicans, the pouch is used to help capture fish, not store fish. Fish are swallowed immediately. On white pelicans, the pouch is so sensitive to touch that they can fish by feel on dark nights. For white and brown pelicans, the pouch is richly endowed with blood vessels that enable pelicans to dissipate body heat by fluttering the pouch. This is called gular fluttering. Pelicans need to maintain the elasticity of the pouch and often stretch it by throwing their heads back or by tucking their head down and turning it inside out on the breast.

cious calories they need over winter or to begin their spring migration north. The more calories they burn, the more food they require to survive. You may not be able to avoid spooking cormorants, which often take flight as soon as they see you. Use a pair of 8x25 binoculars or a camera with a telephoto lens to get a good look at the birds. Also, try to maintain a 90-degree angle to the birds because you cast a much narrower profile, generally making them less likely to fly.

From the log at Comer Key, you have three options. You can paddle due north around the western edge of the two islands in front of you, keeping Jack Daniels Key to your far left, and then hook northeast toward Sandfly Pass. You can take a more direct east/northeast track through the large pass dividing the two unnamed islands just north of Jewell Key and then turn north/northeast to reach Sandfly Pass.

The route here takes a third option to the northeast and then north through a narrow pass dividing the two unnamed islands (one large and one small) in front of you. There are really interesting red mangroves and wonderful wilderness views from the shoreline of the smaller island. As you exit this cut bordered by a fascinating mangrove forest, you will be pointed almost due north, with Jack Daniels Key being the large island to your left. There are a couple of small islands, one off your bow and one directly right. You will bear right around the point to the island to your right and then head east/northeast to Sandfly Pass on your left. You'll probably see boats going up the pass so you'll know you're on the right course.

Because I spent a long time photographing the wrecked western shore of Jewell Key and then admired the white pelicans on Comer Key for quite a while more, I had a strong outgoing tide through Sandfly Pass to contend with on my return trip. It took me two exhausting hours to paddle from the mouth of Sandfly Pass at the Gulf to Chokoloskee Bay. Watch out for crab boats returning to Everglades City who more than likely will not slow for you.

Sandfly Pass splinters into several smaller cuts as it meets Chokoloskee Bay. Choose a side route to avoid the main rush of current. You will be able see the Everglades National Park's Gulf Coast Ranger Station. Set a northeast course of 35 to 40 degrees to reach the canoe ramp.

16. *Picnic and Tiger Keys via West Pass*

Trip highlights: Birds, dolphins, sandy beaches, wide sparkling bays
Charts/maps: Waterproof Chart #40E
Trip rating: Easy to Moderate
Estimated total time: 6 hours
Total distance: 8 nautical miles round trip
Hazards: Muddy launch at low tide, possible brutal wind and tides, some navigational experience required, powerboats in West Pass, particularly past Gaskin Bay
Launch site: Everglades National Park canoe ramp
Ownership: Everglades National Park (239-695-3311)
Alternate routes: Follow Indian Key Pass back to Everglades City from Picnic Key.

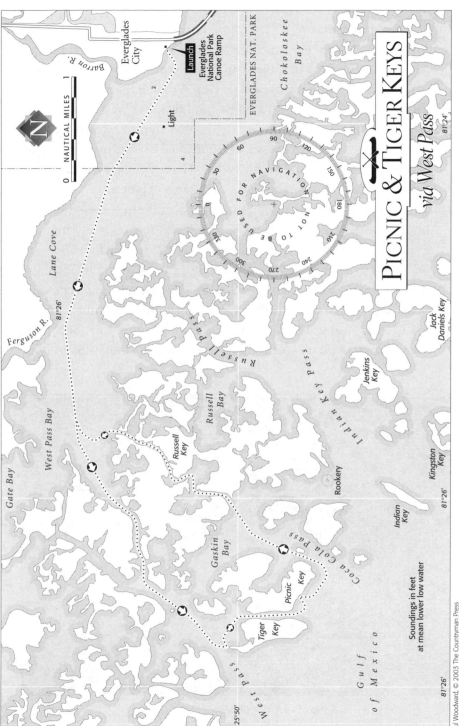

PICNIC & TIGER KEYS
via West Pass

Everglades City

Barron R.

Launch
Everglades
National Park
Canoe Ramp

Light

EVERGLADES NAT. PARK

Chokoloskee
Bay

N
NAUTICAL MILES
0   1

Lane Cove

Ferguson R.

81°26'

Gate Bay

West Pass Bay

Russell Pass

Russell
Bay

Russell
Key

Indian Key Pass

Jenkins
Key

Jack
Daniels Key

81°24'

Gaskin
Bay

Rookery

Kingston
Key

81°26'

Picnic
Key

Coca Cola Pass

Indian
Key

Tiger
Key

West Pass

Gulf
of Mexico

25°50'

81°26'

Soundings in feet
at mean lower low water

USED FOR NAVIGATION TO BE

General Information

The route to Tiger and Picnic Keys via West Pass is an easy to moderate day paddle that also can serve as an easy overnight trip. This trip takes you from the canoe ramp at the Gulf Coast Ranger Station west through Lane Cove to West Pass Bay and then out West Pass to Tiger Key. From Tiger Key it's a quick jaunt around Picnic Key, across Gaskin Bay, to a wide creek that crosses two unnamed bays before leading you back out to West Pass and West Pass Bay. The route then continues back east across Lane Cove to the Gulf Coast Ranger Station.

Overnight paddlers camp by permit on the beautiful sandy shore-lines of both Picnic and Tiger Keys. I have enjoyed many moonlit evenings in this area, and the fishing around Tiger Key for snook and sea trout can be great. At low tide during a day paddle or an overnight trip, take time to explore the expansive mudflats and intimate tidal pools of both islands for crabs, starfish, anemones, and other inverte-brates. West Pass, which skirts the western border of the national park, doesn't seem to carry quite as much boat traffic as Indian, Sandfly, or

A lone red mangrove with cormorants (Gaskin Bay)

Chokoloskee Passes, so you may meet only one or two powerboats until you near the Gulf of Mexico. Dolphins frequent Gaskin Bay and West Pass, so don't be surprised when two or three surface beside you to check you out and then continue on their way.

Access

From US 41 (Tamiami Trail) follow FL 29 for 3 miles south to Everglades City. Continue through town, past the traffic circle, following signs for Everglades National Park and Chokoloskee. Turn right into Everglades National Park. The canoe launch is behind the headquarters and canoe rental.

Route

From the Everglades National Park canoe ramp, head west at about 290 degrees to skirt just to the right of the little island (Totch's Island) near the channel markers for Indian Key Pass. Make certain when you are crossing Chokoloskee Bay and crossing the channels that you do not dally in the channels, either in the Sandfly connector pass or Indian Key Pass. Powerboats have had to idle through the Barron River to your right and they are anxious to get up on plane once they come out of the mouth of the river. Keep an eye out on your right toward the Washingtonian palms on the north side of the airport where there is a pair of bald eagles nesting. Paddle west, keeping Bear Island to your right. At the mouth of the Barron River, about ¾ mile from the boat ramp, look just to the right off your bow to see Lane Cove, which is marked by a point with a channel marker and a boundary of mangrove islets to your left. Continue west at about 310 degrees.

Chokoloskee Bay merges into Lane Cove at the first major point reaching out from the mainland on your right, about 1½ miles from the canoe ramp. From that point head west at about 280 degrees, keeping between the oyster bars and mangrove islets on your left, and keeping the mainland on your right. Stay to your right and use the mainland as a windbreak if the wind is blowing hard from the north or northwest. It will give you some protection. You'll paddle another 1½ miles toward another point on the mainland that marks the end of Lane Cove and the entrance to the Ferguson River.

Some paddlers and many boat captains complain that there isn't much to see in Lane Cove. While that may be true in some cases, during my paddle on a clear Saturday morning in March, the mangrove island chain bordering Lane Cove on my left was at one point draped with pearly strands of egrets that stretched for hundreds of feet. An undulating skein of cormorants crossed my bow and continued northeast, silhouetted against the sky like the shadow of those strands of egrets. A white-phase reddish egret danced after a spray of tiny fish in the shadows of the mangroves in a small cove. Pelicans dove on a large school of mullet. At one point finger mullet started jumping all around my kayak to avoid the snook crashing through them. There was very little boat traffic, particularly for a calm Saturday morning. If you like to fish, I recommend trolling across Lane Cove to spice up your journey.

About 3½ miles from the canoe ramp, you'll pass the mouth of the Ferguson River. The river mouth is not broad and open, but rather a collage of mangrove islands and creeks that meander toward a main channel. It is a spectacular shoreline of oyster bars and jagged mangroves. Continue west (240 degrees) about 1 mile across West Pass Bay to the mouth of West Pass. There are no channel markers, but the channel is apparent, particularly as it quickly narrows. Many of the surrounding mangroves are stained with guano, indicating this is an active bird roost. If you paddle this route in spring, look for swallow-tailed kites soaring just above the tops of the mangroves in search of arboreal lizards and frogs.

After approximately 1½ miles in the pass, you come to a confluence where West Pass meets an unnamed pass draining Gate and Faka-hatchee Bays. As you come around the corner of mangroves at the con-fluence, you can easily see the white sand beach of Tiger Key to your west. Continue at about 210 degrees toward Tiger Key.

Tiger Key is about 5¾ miles from the canoe ramp. The sand spit at the northern tip of the island used to be much more extensive and a popular campsite, but it has eroded away over the years. You may still see campers there though. On the west side of the island, you'll find battered mangroves and expansive mudflats and tidal pools. If you arrive at a tide stage where the mudflats are still exposed, take time to explore them and look for tiny tractorlike tracings left by wandering baby horseshoe crabs, worm trails, shrimp burrows, sea pork (a tunicate that remotely resembles a pork cutlet), and fiddler crabs waving their oversized white claws high as they scuttle en masse toward their burrows in the sand. The male fiddler crabs possess one oversized claw and a small claw. Females bear two feeder claws equal in size.

From the north tip of Tiger Key, paddle southeast at about 130 degrees to brush the eastern side of Tiger Key and enter Coca Cola Pass, which runs between Tiger and Picnic Keys. Picnic Key will be on your left as you enter the pass. Picnic Key also has nice mudflats and a beautiful beach on its south shore, as well as an outhouse. The sea grass flats just off Picnic Key teem with sea trout.

After exploring Picnic Key, paddle around the east side of the island, keeping its shore on your left and passing between it and a small unnamed island on your right. Once you exit the pass between these islands, you'll see a small bay that nearly bisects Picnic Key on your left. Paddle northeast on a heading of about 40 degrees to clear the north shore of Picnic Key, cross Gaskin Bay, and enter an unnamed pass that leads you past the Calusa shell mounds on the western edge of Russell Key. The distance from where you first come around the east side of Picnic Key to the mouth of this pass is about 1 mile. Just beyond the mouth of the pass are the remains of a small shell mound and some dead gumbo limbo trees. Follow the pass as it curves northeast and then north. The pass broadens into a lake on your left. Veer right about 50 degrees into what appears to be another lake, paddle a few hundred feet, and then turn sharply left to follow the pass north/northwest and then northeast as it meanders by Russell Key. Listen for possible mangrove cuckoos as you approach the shell mounds at Russell Key. You'll see the mounds rising to your right beyond the mangroves. Innumerable little mangrove grottos lead away from the pass on the right-hand shore, while the left bank remains relatively unbroken. What's nice about this little pass is not so much that it possesses devastating beauty, but that it is quiet; there is little or no motorboat traffic, and you can

> To understand the shore, it is not enough to catalogue its life. Understanding comes only when, standing on a beach, we can sense the long rhythms of earth and sea that sculpted its land forms and produced the rock and sand of which it is composed; when we can sense with the eye and ear of the mind the surge of life beating always at its shores—blindly, inexorably pressing for a foothold. —Rachel Carson, *The Edge of the Sea*

listen to the prairie warblers calling from somewhere within the mangrove forest. A platter-sized sea turtle surfacing next to your boat and taking a quick gulp of air before it dives toward the bottom in panic may also surprise you. Continue to hug the left shoreline until it breaks to a point, and then head northwest about 310 degrees, keeping to the right of the sandbar about ¼ mile before turning north to return to West Pass as it enters West Pass Bay. Follow a course of about 50 degrees, which is northeast, and then turn more east to paddle back through Lane Cove and Chokoloskee Bay to the canoe ramp. You can use the radio tower at the Everglades City airport as a landmark. Be aware the wind can really come up in the afternoon in the 10,000 Islands, turning Lane Cove and Chokoloskee Bay into a seething washing machine that may push waves over your boat, particularly if the wind and tide are moving in opposite directions. Use a lee shoreline wherever possible to relieve the brunt of the weather.

17. *Halfway Creek/Left-Hand Turner River Loop*

Trip highlights: Birds, dolphins, sandy beaches, wide sparkling bays
Charts/maps: Waterproof Chart #40E
Trip rating: Easy to Moderate
Estimated total time: 6 hours
Total distance: Approximately 8–9 nautical miles round trip
Hazards: Muddy launch at low tide, tour boats on Halfway Creek, possible strong tides and wind, powerboats on lower Turner River, Chokoloskee Bay, and boat canal
Launch site: Everglades National Park canoe ramp
Ownership: Everglades National Park (239-695-3311)
Alternate routes: None

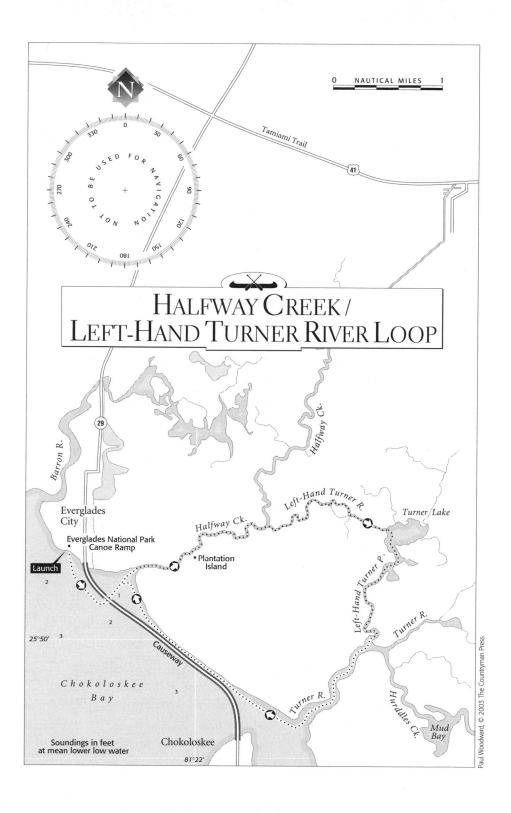

HALFWAY CREEK /
LEFT-HAND TURNER RIVER LOOP

0   NAUTICAL MILES   1

NOT TO BE USED FOR NAVIGATION

Tamiami Trail

41

Halfway Ck.

Barron R.

29

Left-Hand Turner R.

Turner Lake

Everglades
City

Halfway Ck.

Everglades National Park
Canoe Ramp

Launch

Plantation
Island

Left-Hand Turner R.

Turner R.

Causeway

Chokoloskee
Bay

25°50'

Turner R.

Hurddles Ck.

Mud
Bay

Soundings in feet
at mean lower low water

Chokoloskee

81°22'

Paul Woodward, © 2003 The Countryman Press

General Information

Halfway Creek, as its name implies, lies halfway between Barron River and Turner River. In 1892 the first election in the 10,000 Islands was held there amid what are now barely visible cisterns covered mostly over by mangroves. A man brought a ballot box from Key West and according to pioneer Ted Smallwood, "all the poll tax receipts, a jug of licker, a box of cigars. All we had to do was vote."

This loop trip leaves from the Everglades National Park canoe ramp and follows Halfway Creek northeast past a community on Plantation Island before turning into a canopied mangrove creek that loops toward an intersection with Left-Hand Turner River. The route continues on Left-Hand Turner River to Turner Lake, and then follows Left-Hand Turner to Turner River and on to Chokoloskee Bay. It then picks up the boat canal that parallels the causeway from Chokoloskee, passes back under the causeway bridge, and returns to the canoe ramp.

Once past Plantation Island the route becomes wild and lovely. Turner Lake offers good views of osprey nests. Turner River runs past Calusa shell mounds, and even the causeway boat canal offers decent birding.

Access

From US 41 (Tamiami Trail) follow FL 29 for 3 miles south to Everglades City. Continue through town, past the traffic circle, following signs for Everglades National Park and Chokoloskee. Turn right into Everglades National Park. The canoe launch is behind the headquarters and canoe rental.

Route

Start from the Everglades National Park canoe ramp, head southeast to parallel the causeway to Chokoloskee, and then pass under the causeway bridge. Follow the marked channel from the bridge if you are paddling at low water. Otherwise you can cut across and point your bow toward the houses of Plantation Island to the northeast. Plantation Island marks the entrance to Halfway Creek.

Once in the creek you'll pass barnacle-encrusted boats, some houses on pilings, and single- or double-wide trailers with old crab pots for decoration and junk piled on porches and decks. You leave Plantation Island, passing palmettos and a stand of exotic Australian pines, about 2 miles into your trip. The creek at this point is muddy with no canopy and lined by red and black mangroves. At just over 2 miles, you enter Everglades National Park, and Halfway Creek begins to take on a more primordial appearance.

At 2½ miles the canopy begins to close and the light softens as the sun filters through mangrove leaves. Black mangrove pneumatophores extend from the edge of the creek well up the bank, almost like rushes. You can see minnows swimming along the creek edge in the sunlight just below the surface. The creek soon becomes appreciably narrower and begins to twist. Look for drop roots trailing the creek surface from the limbs of some truly majestic red mangroves. If you paddle at a low tide, you sit nearly a foot below the creek bank and inhale a bracing rotten egg stench emanating from the anaerobic mud. You, of course, should be grateful for the aroma because it means you are paddling in verdant mangrove habitat.

At just over 3 miles, you'll encounter a couple of wide spots that offer a place to move out of the way of the tour boat that occasionally plies Halfway Creek. The canopy quickly closes again and you continue paddling through mangrove tunnels. At the junction with Left-Hand Turner River, veer to the east to leave Halfway Creek. The canopy opens up slightly and the river widens and becomes almost boulevard-straight. The river suddenly widens after less than ½ mile and Turner Lake lies before you. Continue east to explore the lake and the osprey nests. You may see flocks of ducks at the extreme east side of the lake. A small creek wriggles away from the northeastern end of the lake, where you may find both black-crowned and yellow-crowned night herons, large tarpon, and even larger alligators. This creek quickly becomes overgrown and tortuous, eventually trickling into a marsh.

To continue on Left-Hand Turner River without exploring the lake, stay to the right and bear south to follow the river as it narrows to about 200 feet wide. The canopy will not close over again. Left-Hand Turner River winds to the southeast and southwest before settling down again

Florida Apple Snail

The Florida apple snail *(Pomacea paludosa)* is a golf ball–sized, brownish, apple-shaped snail common in freshwater rivers, marshes, and sloughs in Big Cypress Swamp and in wetland systems elsewhere in peninsular Florida. It is the largest freshwater snail in North America and 1 among 106 species of apple snails living in tropical and subtropical wetlands worldwide. The most obvious signs of these snails are white egg masses on stalks of vegetation and dead snails bobbing on the water's surface. All apple snails (Family *Ampullaridae*) breathe through a gill that enables the snail to extract oxygen from water; an air sac allows them (through a siphon) to pump oxygen directly from the air above the water surface. Apple snails also use their air sac to regulate their buoyancy in the water column or at the surface.

Apples snail can't form images or see color with their primitive eyes, but they do sense light and darkness. Their tentacles are responsive to tactile and possibly chemical stimuli. The snail's entire body can also sense chemical and mechanical stimuli. Much of the body is made up of a large foot, which enables the snail to move around. Apple snails can move an average of 45 feet a week, but they have been known to move up to 90 feet a day and more than 300 feet in a week. Scientists have been able to track the movements of apple snails from tiny radio transmitters attached to the snails' shells.

Apple snail habitat typically is dominated by emergent vegetation that extends above the water surface so that the snails can climb to breathe, lay eggs, or feed. This includes plants such as cattails, saw grass, and trees such as small cypress and pop ash. Florida apple snails eat grasses, duckweed, bladderworts, and other aquatic vegetation, as well as periphyton, a type of blue-green algae that spreads in dense mats across submerged plants. Periphyton is critical for the snails and other aquatic creatures because it seals in moisture in wetlands during the dry season.

to a general south course. You see large stands of mangroves, occasional cormorants, and tarpon rolling. Paddle about 1½ miles to the confluence with Turner River. Turn right and head southwest. The large complex of Calusa shell mounds will be on the left bank just beyond the next bend. Oyster bars straddle Turner River beyond the shell mounds. At low tide you can easily see them, and at higher tide stages, you may have to look for a riffling S-shape in the water, indicating a bar just below the surface. Fishing for snook, redfish, and sea trout can be very good around the oysters. At the mouth of the Turner River, mangroves

Unlike many other types of snails, Florida apple snails are not hermaphroditic (containing both female and male parts within one animal). A male and female is required for reproduction. Males and females are similar in size and color, differing only slightly in the shape of the shell. After mating, the female climbs up vegetation at night and lays 20–30 wet, soft, pearl-sized eggs that are pink to orange in color and anywhere from a few inches to a couple feet above the water's surface. The eggs soon calcify, turning white and hard. Peak egg-laying occurs in the spring and early summer, which in south Florida may be as early as late January. The eggs hatch after two to three weeks, releasing baby snails that drop into the water at night as miniature replicas of the adults. Apple snails may lay their eggs above the water to avoid having them eaten by aquatic predators and to escape the low oxygen conditions prevalent in wetlands, which could inhibit the development of the embryos.

Apple snails are a food staple for many wetland creatures, including alligators, raccoons, turtles, sunfish (when the snails are tiny), river otters, and many birds. Apple snails are the exclusive food of snail kites and 70 percent of the diet of limpkins, a medium-sized wading bird. The rise and fall of apple snail populations may directly affect the number of snail kites. Based on shells found in shell middens, apple snails may have been popular with the Calusas as well.

Apple snails survive the south Florida dry season by going into a period of dormancy called estivation. A snail seals its shell opening with its operculum, a part of the foot, to prevent the escape of moisture and lies motionless in the marsh for up to four months until water level rises. Baby snails can't survive the dry season, which is why most apple snail eggs, particularly those in marshes that are completely dry down, are laid and hatch after water levels begin to rise. Although the seasonal dry-down may appear hard on the snails, it is critical to prevent emergent vegetation from growing too thick and matted.

have colonized some of the bars. Look for snook around these.

From the mouth of the Turner River, stay to the right and paddle west to follow the boat canal that parallels the causeway. The causeway is constructed entirely of fill dug from the channel that you are paddling. The channel is narrow, and at low tide, you need to hug the shore on the right to stay out of the mud. Yield to motorboats. The canal runs about 1 mile and is a grunt stretch, but the bird-watching can be good. Look for yellow-crowned night herons, spotted sandpipers, belted kingfishers, and various songbirds. Some of the black mangroves along the

Pulling over near the Turner River shell mounds

right shore are majestic. When you approach the causeway bridge, leave the channel only at high water; otherwise you will get stuck in the mud. Once you have passed under the bridge, turn right and paddle about ½ mile northwest back to the Everglades National Park canoe ramp.

The quiet beauty of the Turner River

Part VI
Barron River

The Barron River was named for Barron Collier in 1923 after his purchase of Everglades City. Prior to 1923, the river—much narrower, shallower, and curvaceous than it is today—was known as Allen's River, presumably named after William Allen Smith who homesteaded its banks in 1870 and became Everglades City's first permanent European settler. Before Smith arrived the little river was called Potato Creek because of the potatoes escaped from cultivation that grew along the shore.

Collier set about raising the level of his new town above the reach of high tide by dredging the river, widening, deepening, and straightening it in the process. The river then served as Main Street for several months before roads were built.

You will not notice any labeling of a West Fork and East Fork of the Barron River on navigation charts, but such a designation is necessary in this guide to describe the routes associated with the split in the river that occurs just west of FL 29, at the north end of Everglades City. The West Fork stretches north roughly parallel to FL 29, ending within view of the radio towers at Carnestown on US 41. The East Fork is more extensive, spreading east and terminating as a couple of beautiful lakes, one of which is connected by feeder creeks to upper Halfway Creek. There are three Barron River routes, two of which begin from Everglades City. The third is a loop tour that begins and ends at Seagrape Drive, behind Big Cypress National Preserve headquarters south of US

41. All of the Barron River trips are within the boundaries of Big Cypress National Preserve.

The negative side of the Barron River routes leaving from Everglades City is the incessant roar from airboats, particularly if the wind is blowing from the west/northwest. Airboats are no longer permitted to run on the Barron River within the national preserve, so other than around the marina, where an idle speed is enforced, you won't encounter them while paddling these routes. It is still difficult to escape the noise though. Paddling early (before 9 AM) and late in the day, or with an easterly wind, will help relieve some of this irritation.

18. *Barron River West Fork*

Trip highlights: Varied mangrove and marsh habitat
Charts/maps: Waterproof Chart #40E
Trip rating: Easy
Estimated total time: 4–5 hours
Total distance: 7–8 nautical miles round trip
Hazards: Boat traffic from marina to just east of Barron River Bridge, tricky navigating as river splinters at upper reaches
Launch site: Barron River Marina (ramp fee applies)
Ownership: Big Cypress National Preserve (239-695-4111)
Alternate routes: None

General Information
This is a good trip for beginners because it is short and relatively sheltered from the wind, the tide is generally not too strong, and you don't need a shuttle. It offers a nice introduction to mangrove-lined rivers, intimate creeks, and open marsh.

Access
Follow FL 29 south 3 miles from US 41 to Everglades City. Turn right into the Barron River Marina immediately after crossing the Barron River Bridge. The marina operates a concrete ramp, and a $7 ramp fee applies per vehicle.

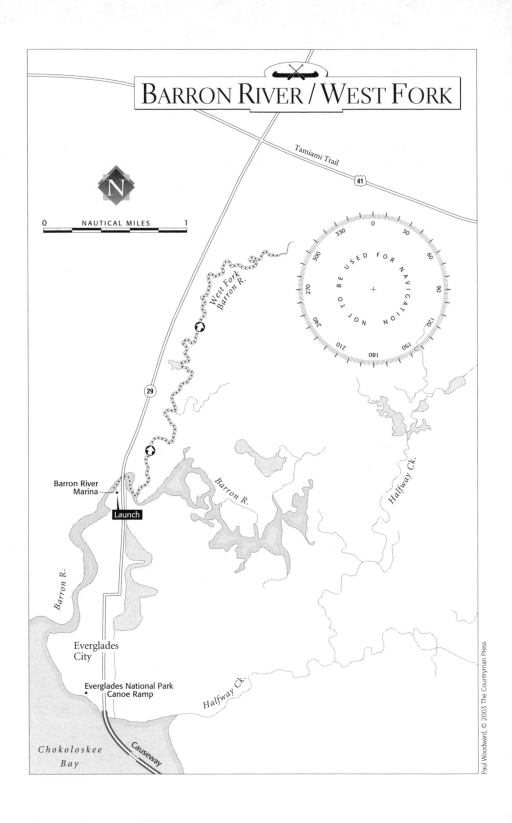

BARRON RIVER / WEST FORK

Tamiami Trail

41

NAUTICAL MILES

0   1

NOT TO BE USED FOR NAVIGATION

0
30
60
90
120
150
180
210
240
270
300
330

West Fork Barron R.

29

Barron River Marina

Launch

Barron R.

Barron R.

Halfway Ck.

Everglades City

Everglades National Park Canoe Ramp

Halfway Ck.

Chokoloskee Bay

Causeway

Paul Woodward, © 2003 The Countryman Press

Route

Launch from Barron River Marina and turn right to paddle under the bridge. Once under the bridge, paddle south down the river, keeping to the left bank to avoid the airboat tour docks. Just past the national park marker, turn left and paddle east/northeast to take the west fork of the river. The noise can be quite loud as airboats run full throttle along the west side of FL 29. Follow the west fork as it winds to the north and slightly east about 1¾ miles to a dead end. Turn right and follow the river as it continues east and then hooks back northwest before opening up into slightly wider water. You'll notice that the mangroves to this point on both sides of the river are denuded to several feet above the water's surface due to prop blast from past airboat use. The river continues to wander from east to northwest at times paralleling FL 29, which is less than ¼ mile to the west. Stay with the main channel as you pass a tunnel wandering off to the right.

Scrubby red mangroves, marsh, and big sky typify the landscape of the upper reaches of the Barron River's West Fork.

At about 2 miles from the marina, you come to a broad opening and continue with the right fork, which will continue taking you north. At a little over 2¼ miles, you have no option but to turn right and head through a little mangrove tunnel, which heads east and then southeast. You soon arrive at a widening in the creek where you can turn right or left. Turn left to paddle northeast. The right turn leads shortly to a dead end.

At just over 2½ miles from the marina, the creek splinters into several braids of water. You may see blue-winged teal on little ponds and swallow-tailed kites hunting over the marsh. Follow these little braids of water as best you can, looking for water flow, which is sluggish at this point, and paddle from east to north until you can go no farther. At about 3¼ miles, you make a turn left to head straight north and should see the steel towers at Carnestown.

This sun-drenched area has the look and feel of traditional Everglades, with wide prairies, scattered cabbage palms, stunted mangroves, wax myrtles, and swamp bays. You'll see what looks like potholes divided by ridges of cordgrass and saw grass. Look for marsh pinks, a beautiful little wildflower, which ranges from pink to white, along the edges of the channels. You will also probably see an occasional white PVC post with green reflector, probably marking an old airboat trail.

To begin your return trip, reverse your route by paddling generally west to southwest. The numerous channels soon become more defined and finally become one as you paddle back downriver. A GPS is useful on this route because there are few places where you lose satellite reception, but do not substitute it for your compass and chart.

There is something very distressing in the gradual passing of the wilds, the destruction of the forests, the draining of the swamps and lowlands, the transforming of the prairies with their wonderful wealth of bloom and beauty, and in its place the coming of civilized man with all his unsightly constructions.…In place of the cries of wild birds there will be heard the …honk of the automobile.…But I wonder quite seriously if the world is any better off because we have destroyed the wilds and filled the land with countless human beings. —Charles Torrey Simpson, *In Lower Florida Wilds*

19. *Barron River East Fork*

Trip highlights: Beautiful wide lakes and great view of
   sunrise/sunset or moonrise
Charts/maps: Waterproof Chart #40E
Trip rating: Easy
Estimated total time: 1½–3 hours
Total distance: About 4 nautical miles round trip
Hazards: Boat traffic from marina to just east of Barron River Bridge,
   possible strong wind on Barron River lakes
Launch site: Barron River Marina (ramp fee applies)
Ownership: Big Cypress National Preserve (239-695-4111)
Alternate routes: None

General Information
This short loop route follows the Barron River east into Big Cypress National Preserve, exploring the various wide meanders and large bays that make up this fork of the river before looping back to your launch at Barron River Marina. This is a great trip to watch the sun rise or set. On full moon evenings you can see sunset and moonrise simultaneously after only 15 minutes paddling from the Barron River Marina. Paddling this route at the beginning or the end of the day should allow you to escape most of the airboat noise.

Access
Follow FL 29 south 3 miles from US 41 to Everglades City. Turn right into the Barron River Marina immediately after crossing the Barron River Bridge. The marina operates a concrete ramp, and a $7 ramp fee applies per vehicle.

Route
Launch from Barron River Marina and turn right to follow the Barron River under the bridge. Stay to the left shore to avoid the airboat tours and follow the river past the national park marker. Do not turn left at the marker or you will be paddling up the West Fork. Follow the East Fork south and east. For the first ½ mile or so, the river will run southeast and

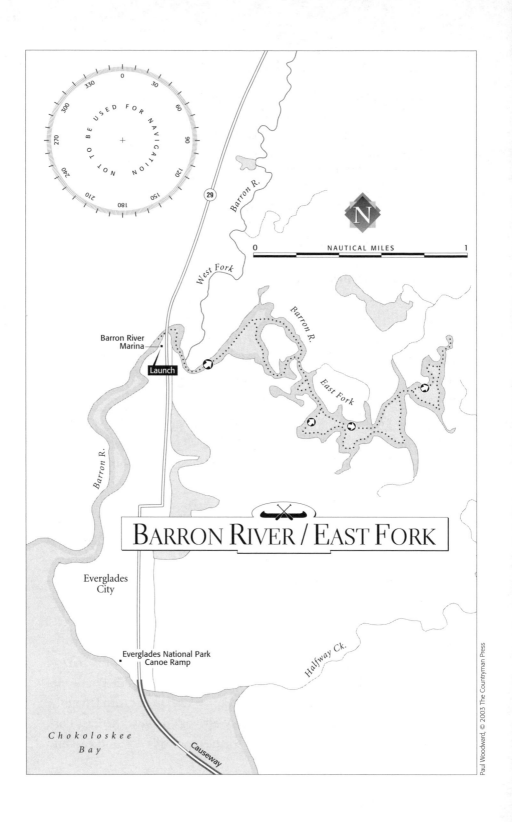

NAUTICAL MILES

BARRON RIVER / EAST FORK

An osprey nest adorns the top of a cabbage palm rising above the Barron River shoreline.

then bend northeast. After paddling east another ¼ mile, you have the choice of turning left and paddling south or continuing easterly. Continue to the east. This confluence (the first large fork in the channels) is an excellent place to watch the sun or moon rise and set. At about 1⅓ miles into your trip, a small bay and creek lead away to the north. On your nautical chart, it appears that this creek should loop back into the main channel, but the tunnel is overgrown and you can't paddle through.

Barron

Just beyond this bay to the east, the Turner River broadens into the first of the big lakes. Paddle around the lakes and explore the edges. There are two connections to Halfway Creek that are covered elsewhere in this guide. On your return trip west back to the marina, paddle on the southern loop channels you passed previously.

20. *Barron River to Seagrape Drive*

Trip highlights: Varied landscape, including beautiful lakes, mangrove creeks, marsh, and the exceptional Halfway Creek

Charts/maps: Waterproof Chart #40E

Trip rating: Moderate to Difficult

Estimated total time: 3–4 hours

Total distance: About 6¼ nautical miles one way

Hazards: Boat traffic from marina to just east of Barron River Bridge, complex navigating between Barron River lakes and Halfway Creek, possible strong wind and tide on Barron River lakes

Launch site: Barron River Marina (ramp fee applies)

Ownership: Big Cypress National Preserve (239-695-4111)

Alternate routes: None

General Information

This route follows the Barron River east into Big Cypress National Preserve and then traces a narrow creek that wriggles erratically northeast and then southeast to Halfway Creek. From Halfway Creek you paddle north up the Seagrape Canal to your take-out at Seagrape Drive. Run this route on the late stages of an incoming tide and ride the current all the way to Seagrape Drive. The national park service has now marked much of this route, making navigation easier.

Access

Follow FL 29 south 3 miles from US 41 to Everglades City. Turn right into the Barron River Marina immediately after crossing the Barron River Bridge. The marina operates a concrete ramp, and a $7 ramp fee applies per vehicle. Leave a vehicle at Seagrape Drive or arrange for a shuttle from Ivey House and NACT-Everglades Rentals and Eco Ad-

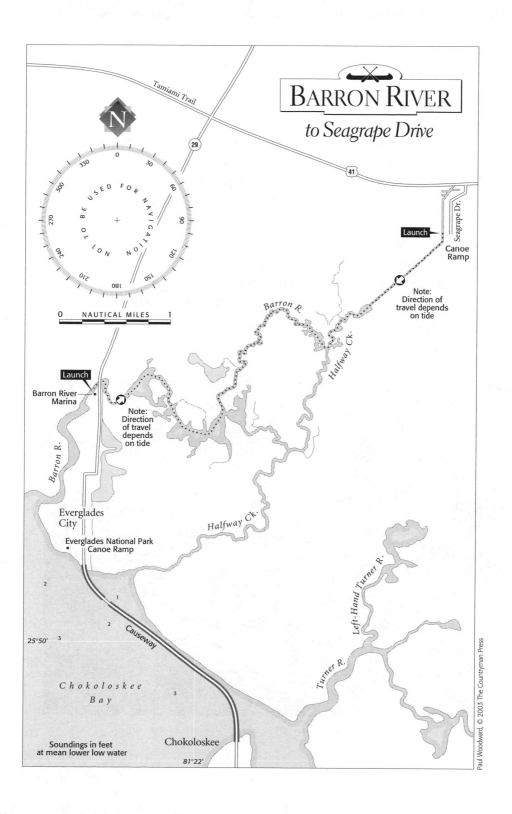

BARRON RIVER
to Seagrape Drive

N

NOT TO BE USED FOR NAVIGATION

0   330   30
300   60
270   90
240   120
210   180   150

0   NAUTICAL MILES   1

Tamiami Trail

29

41

Seagrape Dr.

Launch

Canoe Ramp

Note: Direction of travel depends on tide

Barron R.

Halfway Ck.

Launch

Barron River Marina

Note: Direction of travel depends on tide

Barron R.

Halfway Ck.

Everglades City

Everglades National Park Canoe Ramp

Left-Hand Turner R.

2
1
2
Causeway
25°50'   3

Turner R.

Chokoloskee Bay
3

Chokoloskee

Soundings in feet at mean lower low water

81°22'

Paul Woodward, © 2003 The Countryman Press

ventures if you do not want to paddle back to Everglades City from Sea-grape Drive.

Route

Launch from Barron River Marina and turn right to follow the Barron River under the bridge. Stay to the left shore to avoid the airboat tours and follow the river past the national park marker. Do not turn left at the marker or you will be paddling up the West Fork. Follow the East Fork south and east. The river for the next 1½ miles or so is wide and lightly traveled by motorboats. It broadens into a couple of lovely lakes that are fun to explore, and navigation is straightforward with a chart and compass. Ospreys have built their nests on points in several places along the river. You can easily explore these lakes and then return to Everglades City without worrying too much about getting lost.

Frank Corso paddles a narrowing Barron River on his way to Halfway Creek.

Epiphytes

Epiphytes are plants that rely on other plants as an anchor for survival. Epiphytes manufacture their own food through photosynthesis like other green plants, so they are not parasitic. Epiphytes grow on branches, the trunk, or leaves of a host plant, typically a tree. In some instances they grow in such profusion that they actually crowd out the host plant's leaves or break a limb under their weight. Epiphytes in the Big Cypress Swamp and 10,000 Islands include ferns, bromeliads, and orchids.

Epiphytic ferns include strap ferns, shoelace fern, serpent fern, and resurrection fern, which curls up and turns brown as if dead during periods of little rain only to *resurrect* after a soaking rain, turning green and fluffy again as if it had never appeared any different. Unlike many other ferns, the resurrection fern has no physical means to store water, so it survives by curling up and shutting down until conditions change to its liking.

Bromeliads, or airplants as they are commonly known, are the epiphytes that most paddlers will see during an outing. Thirteen out of the 16 bromeliads native to Florida are found nowhere else in the United States, and one species is found nowhere else in the world. The larger bromeliads, often jutting from the tops of cypress like pineapples on spits, occasionally sport long flower stalks that bloom in the winter or early spring and then set seed. Indeed, pineapples are a variety of bromeliad. Bromeliads are also common in the mangroves, preferring red mangroves, and in particular, buttonwoods because the rough bark offers the perfect site for a tiny bromeliad seed to establish itself and gain a roothold. Hundreds of bromeliads of various species can grow on a single tree. Stiff-leaved wildpine is a large, conspicuous bromeliad that produces stalks with large, beautiful red-and-yellow bracts tipped by tiny blue-and-yellow flowers, usually in February and March.

Most bromeliads take what moisture and nutrients their immediate surroundings provide them, but some have leaves that form a vaselike structure at the center of the plant, helping trap airborne detritus and store water. The mini-ecosystem that develops within the protected vase, or tank, includes algae and microscopic crustaceans, in addition to insect larvae, spiders, frogs, and in the tropics, even species of crabs. Beneficial bacteria and fungi help break down the materials that fall into the tanks, which enable nutrients to be more easily absorbed by the plant.

One type of bromeliad found in the Big Cypress Swamp, *Catopsis berteroniana,* is thought to be carnivorous. It produces a waxy powder at the base of the leaves, and to some extent, on the blades of the leaves to trap flying insects. The powder reflects ultraviolet light and may confuse insects into mistaking the bromeliad leaves for open sky, causing them to crash into the center of the plant. The powder is also slippery, which may prevent the stunned insects from crawling out of the water and decaying organic matter at the center of the plant.

Another bromeliad common throughout the Southeast, but rarely thought of by most folks as an airplant, is Spanish moss. Spanish moss bears long gray strands made up of slender, threadlike, greenish-gray limbs coated with tiny scales that absorb water. It even produces tiny, greenish-white flowers.

Orchids are the starlets of the epiphyte world, although not all orchids are epiphytes (neither are all ferns and bromeliads). Florida's epiphytic orchids are generally small, usually inconspicuous, and rarely as showy as commercial varieties coveted by orchid fanciers. The ghost orchid, night-scented orchid, and clamshell orchid, among the most beautiful of the south Florida native orchids, are generally found deep within freshwater swamps, so the chances of seeing them on any of these routes are slim. The orchids that you may see if you look closely among the mangroves, usually in areas with few bromeliads, include the rigid epidendrum, and in less shaded areas, the Florida butterfly orchid. Both of these orchids are lovely, particularly if you observe the flowers with a magnifying glass.

Remember that virtually all of the orchid species in south Florida and many bromeliads are endangered, primarily from past over-collecting, so do not take them home with you. It is illegal, and the plant will more than likely die. Wild orchids, in particular, are very specific about the conditions under which they will survive. Most orchids and bromeliads in south Florida are tropical by origin and can't tolerate large variations in temperature, light levels, and humidity. Even breaking or cutting limbs in order to see them better can threaten their chances of survival by increasing their exposure to lower humidity and direct sunlight, and their vulnerability to frost.

As you paddle north at the top of the large lake where it begins to narrow to a creek, do not turn right to paddle into the lake to your east (at about the 1½ miles from the marina) if you plan to continue on this route to Seagrape Drive. Follow the creek north. If your timing is good, you will be riding an incoming tide as it rips through this creek, carrying you along at a good pace. (*Note:* At this point you intersect the Halfway Creek/Barron River Loop, which is route 9). Turn right into this lake and reverse the directions found for that route for an alternate paddle tour to Seagrape Drive.

After about ½ mile from where you entered the creek at the lake, you will see another creek leading away on your left. Stay right and continue on your current route as it bends slightly northeast. After a few hundred feet, a tunnel leads away to the right. It is a dead end. Your route will veer north and then northwest and then wriggle along on a generally north path. Paddle ¼ mile to another tiny pond. You will have paddled about 3 miles from the marina at this point. Head northwest into a mangrove tunnel. The creek is very narrow, and after a few hundred feet, the canopy alternately breaks and closes several times. You are headed basically northeast. You will see buttonwood trees with beautiful airplants, arthritis vine, and candy coral on the mangrove roots, which looks like silly string. These are all indicators that you are traveling in relatively fresh water.

At 3¼ miles from the marina, the creek splits. Stay to the left. You will probably see a marker at this junction, although it gives no indication of which direction you should go (don't trust the direction the beer can may be pointing). Continue paddling through a narrow yet open creek with no canopy. At 3½ miles you arrive at another pond and then swing around a bend to the southeast. You travel another ³⁄₁₀ mile to a point where you need to make a turn to the northeast, following the current rather than staying on the southeast course. You pass three cabbage palms, one significantly taller than the others, growing close to the water's edge. Travel ³⁄₁₀ mile to another pond, where there is another choice to go north or east. Take the route that brings you more to the east because you have begun your southeast descent into the bays of Halfway Creek. Paddle another few hundred feet and come to another pond; you continue southeast through more ponds ringed with cabbage palms and mangroves.

At just over 4 miles from the marina, you approach a cabbage palm with a pileated woodpecker hole near the top; come around the bend and look for a cabbage palm growing low over the creek adorned with serpent ferns in its boots. Continue east from this cabbage palm. After just under ¼ mile from the cabbage palm, you arrive at the first of the Halfway Creek bays. You are about 4¼ miles from your launch at the marina. Paddle southeast across the bays at 150 degrees.

The bays, while not huge, are fairly wide and lined by scrubby man-

> Is it any wonder then that with the fierce competition for space, light, and opportunity in the forests the weaker plants are driven out into the swamps, into the water, or onto the trees to live as epiphytes; anywhere that they can find room and make out an existence? Is it strange that they seem to resort to all kinds of schemes which will give their seeds a chance to grow and reproduce their species? —Charles Torrey Simpson, *In Lower Florida Wilds*

groves, beyond which grow cordgrass and plenty of cabbage palms. You pass a tiny island close to the bank on your left with a cabbage palm, a couple of snags, and huge bromeliads growing in the center. Paddle to the east end of the bay and through a little connector creek about 20 feet long. This drops you into Halfway Creek at marker 3. Turn left to paddle northeast up Halfway Creek. Halfway Creek is absolutely beautiful, with tall cabbage palms and many buttonwood trees adorned with epiphytic orchids and bromeliads. Pass a marker on the northwest side of the river. There is another waterway going off to the east that leads you to a dead end.

You pass marker 2 at about 5 miles from the marina. Once you come around marker 1, you'll see the Seagrape Canal in front of you across a little bay. This little bay marks the headwaters of Halfway Creek. Follow the canal about 1 mile to the canoe launch at Seagrape Drive.

Osprey in flight

Part VII

Chokoloskee

Chokoloskee Island marks the end of FL 29 and the farthest point south you can drive in the 10,000 Islands. Chokoloskee Bay, which completely surrounds Chokoloskee Island, is 10 miles long by about 2 miles wide and no more than 5 feet deep. Until 1900, Chokoloskee, meaning old house in Seminole, was used to describe the entire region touching the bay.

Extensive Calusa shell mounds covered much of Chokoloskee Island, providing high ground for settlement and fertile soil for agriculture on the 150-acre island. Settlers on the island primarily farmed, fished, and hunted for their livelihood. Fruit groves were successful. A few folks tried ideas somewhat more far-fetched. The Lopez brothers, responding with typical 10,000 Islands pioneer ingenuity to the demand for wading bird plumes in the early 1900s, experimented in 1915 with a plume bird ranch by taking wading birds chicks from the nest and hand-feeding them. Whether the birds were to be killed or merely stripped of their ornamental feathers is not known. The birds apparently required too much food, and the Lopez brothers abandoned their scheme.

C.G. McKinney and Ted Smallwood were two of the island's most prominent citizens. McKinney, known as the Sage of the Everglades, was the closest thing to a doctor the island was to see for years, and he was instrumental in getting the island a post office by 1891. He wrote about current news on Chokoloskee Island for the local paper, and it is his writing that sheds considerable insight into the fortitude required to merely survive in the islands. In 1925 he reported about the foundering school, "Our school is moving slowly being somewhat crippled up, the swamp angels (mosquitoes) being so fearful just now. It is hard to run anything here now except a spray gun."

Ted Smallwood succeeded McKinney as postmaster and was the island's primary landowner in the early 1900s. He was also perhaps the region's most successful store owner. Take time to visit the Smallwood Store, a historic trading post and museum, but don't launch your boat there, despite the tempting beach. Their parking is extremely limited.

The causeway linking Chokoloskee to Everglades City dates back to 1954 and was paved in 1956. There are a couple of good places to launch on both sides of the road, but they can be muddy at low tide. A sidewalk now runs along the east side of the causeway; so if you launch from that side, chances are you will need to park on the west side of the road so you don't block the sidewalk. Make certain you don't park in a No Parking zone as well.

As with paddle trips originating from Everglades City, time your departures here to take advantage of an outgoing tide to carry you to the Gulf of Mexico and an incoming tide to bring you back to the island.

21. *Rabbit Key via the Auger Hole and Rabbit Key Pass*

Trip highlights: Sandy beach, wide sparkling bays, interesting passes, possible dolphin and sea turtle sightings

Charts/maps: Waterproof Chart #40E

Trip rating: Moderate to Difficult

Estimated total time: 5–7 hours round trip

Total distance: About 12 nautical miles round trip

Hazards: Possible strong wind and tide, oyster bars, motorboat traffic in Rabbit Key Pass, lots of open water, somewhat tricky navigation

Launch site: Chokoloskee causeway or Outdoor Resorts canoe ramp (fee required for canoe ramp)

Ownership: Everglades National Park (239-695-3311)

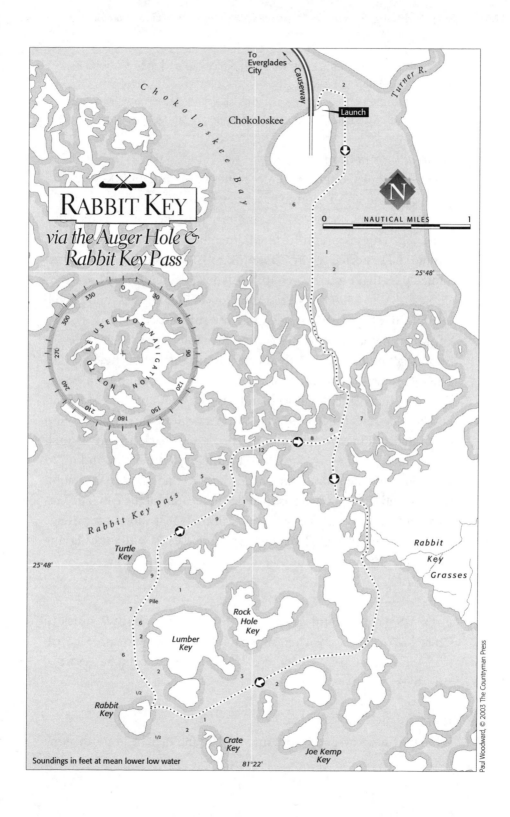

RABBIT KEY
*via the Auger Hole &
Rabbit Key Pass*

To
Everglades
City

Causeway

Chokoloskee

Launch

Turner R.

Chokoloskee Bay

N

0   NAUTICAL MILES   1

25°48'

NOT TO BE USED FOR NAVIGATION

Rabbit Key Pass

Turtle
Key

25°48'

Rabbit
Key
Grasses

Rock
Hole
Key

Lumber
Key

Pile

Rabbit
Key

Crate
Key

Joe Kemp
Key

Soundings in feet at mean lower low water   81°22'

Paul Woodward, © 2003 The Countryman Press

Alternate routes: Leave from Chokoloskee and follow Rabbit Key
Pass to Rabbit Key.
Depending on tide and wind, this alternate route may range from
easy to difficult, although navigation is straightforward.

General Information

There are simpler and more direct routes to reach Rabbit Key's pretty
little beach, but if you want to practice your navigational skills and see
more interesting scenery with less motorboat traffic, you will enjoy this
route. The trip takes you from a launch beside the causeway south
around the eastern edge of Chokoloskee Island and through an unnamed pass that bisects a group of islands (also unnamed) south of
Chokoloskee to Rabbit Key Pass. You cross Rabbit Key Pass and paddle
south into a bay with a jagged, narrow cut in its southeast corner
known locally as the Auger Hole. You then follow the Auger Hole out
into a shallow, narrow bay that leads toward the Rabbit Key Grasses.
The route skirts to the north of Rabbit Key Grasses, rounds an exten-
sion of the mainland to cut west and pass just south of Rock Hole and
Lumber Keys, and finally skims north of Crate Key to reach Rabbit Key.
From Rabbit Key you take a more direct path back to your launch
point, tracking along the northwest shore of Lumber Key and on to
Turtle Key, and then completing a loop back to Chokoloskee via Rabbit
Key Pass and the unnamed pass paddled at the start of the trip. The Waterproof Chart #40E is the only practical chart that shows the passage
through the Auger Hole. Time this trip to paddle out with the outgoing
tide and return on the incoming tide.

Access

From US 41 (Tamiami Trail), take FL 29 south about 7 miles to
Chokoloskee. Park somewhere along the causeway to launch, or launch
from the mud ramp at Outdoor Resorts. Outdoor Resorts charges a $10
launch fee.

Route

From the causeway, paddle out into the bay and then head south along the east shoreline of Chokoloskee Island. There are ruins and extensive oyster bars extending from the southern tip of Chokoloskee Island. If you are paddling at a high tide so that the oysters are well covered, set a course of 160–170 degrees from the tip of the island and paddle about ¾ mile into a pass. If you are paddling at low tide, stay to the east (left) of the oysters, paddle south about the same distance, and then correct your course to the southwest once you are past the shoals.

From this point, there are four small passes that connect to Rabbit Key Pass, none of which have names on the charts. These directions follow the easternmost pass, which you can identify on Waterproof Chart #40E as the one from which two mangrove points flare out from either side like legs. If you miss this pass, but catch the next one, they merge. The other two take you close to the same point on Rabbit Key Pass, but you have to deal with motorboat traffic (as indicated by the solid line on your Waterproof Chart #40E).

This eastern pass splits as it swirls around a little island (you can paddle around the island either direction) and continues generally southeast, making a sharp hook east about midway through its course toward Rabbit Key Pass. It is quite serene and shallow with a sand bottom and numerous oyster bars. Listen for white-eyed vireos and prairie warblers in the mangroves. Once you exit this pass, look south for channel markers and/or boats indicating Rabbit Key Pass. At this point you have paddled roughly 3 miles.

There is a beautiful sandbar right at Rabbit Key Pass that you need to skirt (or get out and stretch your legs) if you are paddling at low tide. Paddle south at about 180–190 degrees from the channel marker (this channel marker apparently does not appear on navigation charts) and sandbar to the far end of the bay and the Auger Hole, which is on your left. The Auger Hole is the local name for this quiet little creek through the mangroves that connects you to the bays of the Rabbit Key Grasses. The entrance to the Auger Hole is guarded by a snaggle-toothed bar of razor-sharp oysters, so use extreme caution if you must portage this area due to low water. Paddle through the short, winding Auger Hole; and when you pop out into a small pond, set a course of about 130 degrees into a bay toward the eastern mangrove shoreline about ¼ mile

Horseshoe crabs mating in the shallows of Robert Key

away. As you approach the shore, the shallow, muddy bay curves back to the south. Over the next ½ mile, you pass a mangrove creek wriggling off to the east and a constriction of the bay as it opens into a much larger bay. On some charts the whole large bay in front of you is denoted as Rabbit Key Grasses, but on the Waterproof Chart #40E, Rabbit Key Grasses refers only to the small eastern corner of the bay.

From here, continue paddling south about ¾ mile, passing one point of the mainland on your right and then keeping to your right, making the southern tip of the mainland. A maze of islands will confront you. As you come around the point, you can see Lumber and Rock Hole Keys to the west (right). This is a good area to see dolphins. Set a course of about 250 degrees west and paddle about 1¼ miles across open water to reach Rabbit Key, keeping Lumber and Rock Hole Keys to your right. When you near the south end of Lumber Key, you'll easily be able to identify Rabbit Key by its white sandy beach. If a strong sea breeze kicks up from the south, try ducking into the pass separating Lumber and Rock Hole Keys, paddling north through the pass, and then turning left to continue west and south in the lee of Lumber Key to reach Rabbit Key. A large sandbar nearly joins Lumber and Rabbit Keys at low tide. The sandbar is covered at high tide, and motorboats may pass here between the two islands.

Rabbit Key is perfect for a nice lunch in the shade of mangroves, sunning on the sand, and watching horseshoe crabs come ashore at high tide to mate on the beach at your feet. There is an outhouse, and camping is allowed by backcountry permit from Everglades National Park. If you tire of the beach, you can explore the little creek that cuts across Lumber Key's southern end.

To begin your return to Chokoloskee, paddle north from Rabbit Key on a course of about 350 degrees past the northwest tip of Lumber Key, and then continue north at about 15 or 20 degrees to pass inside the east shore of Turtle Key. If you are lucky, you may glimpse a sea turtle surface, gasp for air, its head completely exposed, and then quickly submerge as you paddle past Turtle Key. You generally will not see it surface again.

Once you pass Turtle Key, stay just to the south of Rabbit Key Pass

> Once I discovered a curious little mollusk living in a meadow of turtle grass on the floor of a quiet bay among Florida's 10,000 Islands. It was the same bright green as the grass, and its little body was much too large for its thin shell, out of which it bulged. It was one of the scaphanders, and its nearest living relatives are inhabitants of the Indian Ocean.
> —Rachel Carson, *The Edge of the Sea*

to avoid boat traffic and take advantage of the lee from the mainland on your right, continuing on a northeast course. You'll pass a small island or two on your left. Rabbit Key Pass narrows and turns to the east about 1 mile from Turtle Key, and you'll want to turn sharply north to meet it. Paddle east in Rabbit Key Pass on a heading of about 80 degrees until you reach the channel marker you left earlier in the day to reach the Auger Hole. Turn northeast back into the pass. Once you exit the pass, Chokoloskee is plainly visible to the north, and you continue back to your point of entry on Chokoloskee.

22. No Name Mangrove Tunnel and Island Wilderness Loop

Trip highlights: Mangrove tunnel, wide sparkling bays, interesting passes, possible dolphin and sea turtle sightings
Charts/maps: Waterproof Chart #40E
Trip rating: Moderate
Estimated total time: 4¼–5 hours round trip
Total distance: 9 nautical miles round trip
Hazards: Possible strong wind and tide, oyster bars, motorboat traffic in Rabbit Key Pass, some open water, somewhat tricky navigation
Launch site: Chokoloskee causeway or Outdoor Resorts canoe ramp (fee required for canoe ramp)
Ownership: Everglades National Park (239-695-3311)
Alternate routes: None

General Information
The No Name Mangrove Tunnel and Island Wilderness Loop is a scenic

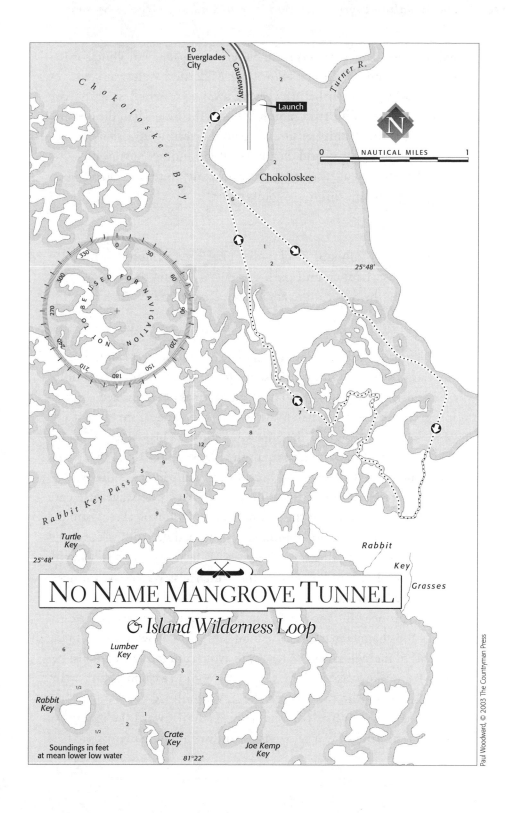

To Everglades City

Causeway

Launch

Chokoloskee Bay

Chokoloskee

N

0   1
NAUTICAL MILES

Turner R.

2

2

6

2

1

2

25°48'

NOT TO BE USED FOR NAVIGATION

0
330
30
300
60
270
90
240
120
210
150
180

Rabbit Key Pass

7

8
6

12

9

5

1

9

Turtle
Key

25°48'

Rabbit

Key

Grasses

NO NAME MANGROVE TUNNEL
& Island Wilderness Loop

Lumber
Key

6

2

3

2

Rabbit
Key

1/2

1

2

1/2

2

Crate
Key

Joe Kemp
Key

Soundings in feet
at mean lower low water

81°22'

Paul Woodward, © 2003 The Countryman Press

half-day paddle that begins from either the causeway or Outdoor Resorts canoe ramp. The route follows the Wilderness Waterway south toward the Lopez River before veering away to a nameless mangrove tunnel just west of the river mouth. It tracks the tunnel half the distance to its exit at the Rabbit Key Grasses before diverting up a shallow lake, across Rabbit Key Pass, and then north along another narrow pass that meanders though a cluster of nameless islands south of Chokoloskee. Can you guess how this route got its name?

Access
From US 41 (Tamiami Trail), take FL 29 south about 7 miles to Chokoloskee. Launch and park somewhere along the causeway, or launch from the canoe ramp at Outdoor Resorts.

Route
Paddle south/southeast from the causeway (east or west side), or from the canoe ramp at Outdoor Resorts, toward the southeastern tip of Chokoloskee Island, which on nautical charts is often marked *ruins,* to intersect with the Wilderness Waterway. If you paddle from the east side of the causeway, you pass the Smallwood Store, a historic trading post and museum, at the southern tip of the island. At the tip of the island, set a course of 130 degrees southeast to gradually intersect the Wilderness Waterway. If you are paddling at a lower tide stage, use care skirting the oyster bars at the southern end of Chokoloskee. From the west side of the island and Outdoor Resorts, paddle southeast at about 140 degrees, intersecting the Wilderness Waterway more directly, with the mainland at your left. Follow the Wilderness Waterway southeast toward the Lopez River.

As you near the mouth of the Lopez River, you pass a series of shoals and channel markers for Rabbit Key Pass. At low tide stick to the channel of the Wilderness Waterway to avoid running aground. Just beyond Rabbit Key Pass, look to your right and find a chain of little mangroves jutting from the western shore. Veer toward those mangroves and then keep south as you paddle into a bay toward the mangrove shoreline in front of you, allowing the little chain of mangroves to pass close on your right. As you approach the edge of the bay, you'll see the entrance to the mangrove tunnel. The Lopez River is off to your east. The mouth of the tunnel is about 3½ miles from your launch site.

Enter the mangrove tunnel and follow it south. At high tide the water is a milky, murky brown and the canopy is high and not complete. You may hear the roar of the sea breeze blowing over the canopy. Regardless of what tide you're on, the current flowing through the tunnel should not pose a problem. The tunnel is peaceful, and you pass some grand old black and red mangroves, with mangrove crabs spilling off their branches. You may also see small, air-breathing mangrove periwinkle snails. Small feeder creeks circle away from the pass on your left and then intersect a short distance from where they departed from the main creek.

After paddling about ½ mile through the tunnel, you come to a little donut where you can paddle either way around an island. The path to the west is the most open and easiest to paddle. Continue paddling south down the channel after it becomes one again. A short distance later, you are faced with the choice of continuing south down the tunnel toward Rabbit Key Grasses or turning right (northwest) to pass under a beautiful mangrove arch and into a wide, shallow lake. There are a couple of ways to exit the lake, one along the east shore and one along the west shore, and you may have to choose based on which offers the most water. At dead low tide there is a narrow channel snaking toward the west shore you can follow to exit to Rabbit Key Pass.

If you have enough water, stay to the east shore and paddle northwest across the lake, through a pass, and then out into the wider water of Rabbit Key Pass. Paddle north to the opposite shore of Rabbit Key Pass, and then follow the shoreline east for a couple hundred yards or so to a creek entering from the mangroves on your left. Turn left and paddle into a lovely creek. This short creek, narrow at first, widens, narrows, and then widens again as it turns to the southwest and opens into a bay. Turn left to paddle southwest toward Rabbit Key Pass; and then at the near edge of the channel, sharply round a small island (there is a channel marker at the point) and paddle 300 degrees northwest for about ½ mile to intersect a pass that will lead you back to Chokoloskee

Curtains of rain fall from a storm over Chokoloskee Bay

Bay. You can get back to Chokoloskee by following any of the passes leading north or northwest in this area, so if you miss this one, it's not a big deal.

After you enter the pass, it turns sharply north, widens, and divides around a small island before coming together as one again. It's easiest to stay to the right, as the pass veers sharply west and then swings back to the northwest and north, as you approach Chokoloskee Bay. From the mouth of the pass, look north across Chokoloskee Bay to Chokoloskee Island and set your course to your launch site on the island.

Appendix

Government Agencies

Big Cypress National Preserve (Ochopee Visitor Center)
239-695-1201/239-695-4111
www.nps.gov/bicy/
(Ochopee Visitor Center is located halfway between Naples and Miami on US 41)

Everglades National Park (Gulf Coast Visitor Center)
239-695-3311/305-242-7740 (emergency dispatcher)
www.nps.gov/ever/
(Everglades City, at the edge of Chokoloskee Bay)

10,000 Islands National Wildlife Refuge
239-353-8442
southeast.fws.gov/TenThousandIsland/index.htm
(No visitors center)

Rookery Bay National Estuarine Research Reserve
300 Tower Road
Naples, FL 34113
239-417-6310
www.rookerybay.org

Collier-Seminole State Park
20200 East Tamiami Trail
Naples, FL 33961
239-394-3397
www.dep.state.fl.us/parks/district4/collier-seminole/index.asp

(Camping reservations from Reserve America at 800-326-3521)

Fakahatchee Strand State Preserve
P.O. Box 548
Copeland, FL 33926
239-695-4593
www.dep.state.fl.us/parks/district4/Fakahatcheestrand/index.asp

Visitor Information

Everglades City and Chokoloskee

Everglades City Chamber of Commerce
P.O. Box 130
Everglades City, FL 33929
239-695-3941/1-800-226-9609
www.florida-everglades.com

Lodging

Barron River Motel, Marina, and RV Park
P.O. Box 116
Everglades City, FL 32139
239-695-3331/1-800-535-4961
www.evergladespark.com

Everglades City Motel
310 Collier Avenue
Everglades City, FL 34139
239-695-4224/1-800-695-8353

Ivey House B&B and Guest Inn
P.O. Box 5038, 107 Camellia Street
Everglades City, FL 34139
239-695-3299
www.iveyhouse.com

(Guests save 20 percent on canoe and kayak rentals; the B&B has shared bath and the Guest Inn has large rooms, private baths, and access to swimming pool)

On the Banks of the Everglades
P.O. Box 570, 201 West Broadway
Everglades City, FL 34139
239-695-3151/1-888-431-1977
www.banksoftheeverglades.com
(Offers B&B, suites, and efficiencies)

Outdoor Resorts
P.O. Box 429
Chokoloskee Island, FL 34138
239-695-3788/239-695-2881
(RV park, motel, marina, and canoe ramp)

Dining

Rod and Gun Club
200 Riverside Drive, Everglades City
239-695-2101
(Serves dinner)

The Captain's Table Lodge and Villas
102 East Broadway, Everglades City
239-695-4211/1-800-741-6430

Everglades Seafood Depot
102 Collier Avenue, Everglades City
239-695-0075
(Serves lunch and dinner)

Ghost Orchid Grill at the Ivey House
107 Camellia Street, Everglades City
239-695-3299
(Serves breakfast, lunch, and dinner; Wednesday night speaker series

from December through April, and a full gourmet menu including vege-tarian entrees)

JT's Island Grill and Gallery
238 Mamie Street, Chokoloskee Island
239-695-3633

(Serves lunch daily and dinner on Tuesday, Friday, and Saturday only)

Oar House Restaurant
305 Collier Avenue, Everglades City
239-695-3535

(Serves breakfast, lunch, and dinner)

Oyster House
Across from Everglades National Park, Everglades City
239-695-2073

(Serves lunch and dinner)

Guides/Rentals

NACT-Everglades Rentals and Eco Adventures
Located at the Ivey House
239-695-3299/239-695-4666

(Rents canoes and kayaks, including single, double, sit-on-top, and tradi-tional; offers guided half- and multi-day backcountry tours November through April, as well as shuttles, private dock, and skiff tours)

Everglades National Park Boat Tours
Gulf Coast Visitor Center, Everglades City
239-695-2591/1-800-445-7724 (in Florida)

(Rents 17-foot Grumman canoes only for day and overnight)

JT's Island Grill and Gallery
238 Mamie Street, Chokoloskee Island
239-695-3633

(Rents single and double kayaks and offers limited shuttle service)

Outdoor Resorts
P.O. Box 429
Chokoloskee Island, FL 34138
239-695-3788/239-695-2881

(Rents sit-on-top kayaks and offers a canoe ramp but fee applies)

Tamiami Trail

Dining

Joanie's Blue Crab Café
39395 Tamiami Trail, Ochopee
239-695-2682

Camping

Collier-Seminole State Park
20200 East Tamiami Trail
Naples, FL 33961
239-394-3397/1-800-326-3521 (reservations from Reserve America)

Big Cypress National Preserve
239-695-1201/239-695-4111

(Park service campgrounds available at Burns Lake, Monument Lake, Dona Drive, and Midway)

Big Cypress Trail Lakes Campground
Tamiami Trail
Ochopee, FL 33943
239-695-2275

Marco Island/Goodland

Marco Island Chamber of Commerce
1102 North Collier Boulevard
Marco Island, FL 34145

239-394-7549

(Can help you with lodging and dining choices in the area)

Port of the Islands

Lodging

Port of the Islands Condominium-Hotel Resort
25000 Tamiami Trail East
Naples, FL 34114
239-394-3101
www.portoftheislands.com

Dining

Manatee Market Bar & Grill
25000 Tamiami Trail East
Naples, FL 34114
239-394-3101

(Lunch and dinner Wednesday through Saturday; brunch only on Sunday)

Camping

Port of the Islands RV Resort
12425 Union Road
Naples, FL 34114
239-642-5343/1-800-319-4447
www.portoftheislands.com

Guided Kayak Tours

Acadia 1 Watersports
184 High Street, #174
Ellsworgh, ME 04605
1-888-786-0676
www.kayak1.com

Tide and Weather Information

www.co-ops.nos.noaa.gov
(Tide information; click on predictions *and then follow instructions)*

www.noaa.gov
(Direct National Weather Service forecast, marine conditions, and radar imagery without advertising)

www.weather.com
(Weather information from The Weather Channel)

Suggested Reading

Natural History

Carr, Archie. *The Everglades.* 1973. New York: Time-Life Books.

Carson, Rachel. *The Edge of the Sea.* 1983. Boston: Houghton Mifflin Company.

Elphick, Chris, John B. Dunning, Jr., and David Allen Sibley, editors. *The Sibley Guide to Bird Life and Behavior.* 2001. New York: Chanticleer Press, Inc.

Farren, Rick. *The Longstreet Highroad Guide to the Florida Keys & Everglades.* 1999. Atlanta: Longstreet Press. (limited availability, full text at www.sherpaguides.com/florida/index.html)

Fergus, Charles. *Swamp Screamer: At Large with the Florida Panther.* 1998. Gainesville: University Press of Florida.

Ripple, Jeff. *Florida: The Natural Wonders.* 1997. Stillwater, MN: Voyageur Press.

Ripple, Jeff. *Manatees and Dugongs of the World.* 1999. Stillwater, MN: Voyageur Press.

Ripple, Jeff. *Southwest Florida's Wetland Wilderness.* 1996. Gainesville: University Press of Florida.

Simpson, Charles Torrey. *In Lower Florida Wilds.* 1920. New York: G.P. Putnam's Sons.

Toops, Connie. *The Florida Everglades.* 1998. Stillwater, MN: Voyageur Press.

History

Tebeau, Charlton W. *Florida's Last Frontier: This History of Collier County.* 1966. Miami: University of Miami Press.

Tebeau, Charlton W. *Man in the Everglades: 2000 Years of Human History in Everglades National Park.* 1968. Miami: University of Miami Press.

Tebeau, Charlton W. *The Story of Chokoloskee Bay Country.* 1976. Miami: Banyon Books.

Literature

Cerulean, Susan, editor. *The Book of the Everglades.* 2002. Minneapolis: Milkweed Editions.

Matthiessen, Peter. *Killing Mr. Watson.* 1991. New York: Vintage Books.

Oppel, Frank, and Tony Meisel, editors. *Tales of Old Florida.* 1987. Secaucus, NJ: Castle.

Field Guides

Amos, William H., and Stephen H. *Atlantic and Gulf Coasts. The Audubon Society Nature Guides.* 1985. New York: Alfred A. Knopf, Inc.

Glassberg, Jeffrey, Marc C. Minnow, and John V. Calhoun. *Butterflies through Binoculars: A Field, Finding, and Gardening Guide to Butterflies in Florida.* 2000. Oxford: Oxford University Press.

Kaplan, Eugene H. *Southeastern and Caribbean Seashores.* 1988. Peterson Field Guides. Boston: Houghton-Mifflin Company.

National Geographic Society. *Field Guide to the Birds of North America.* 1987. Washington: National Geographic Society.

Nelson, Gill. *The Shrubs and Woody Vines of Florida.* 1996. Sarasota, FL: Pineapple Press.

Nelson, Gill. *The Trees of Florida.* 1994. Sarasota, FL: Pineapple Press.

Taylor, Walter Kingsley. *Florida Wildflowers in Their Natural Communities.* 1998. Gainesville: University Press of Florida.

Paddling Guides

Alderson, Doug. *Sea Kayaker's Savvy Paddler: More Than 500 tips for Better Kayaking.* 2001. Camden, NJ: Ragged Mountain Press/Mc-Graw-Hill.

Foster, Nigel. *Guide to Sea Kayaking in Southern Florida.* 1999. Old Saybrook, CT: The Globe Pequot Press.

Molloy, Johnny. *A Paddler's Guide to Everglades National Park.* 2000. Gainesville, FL: University Press of Florida.

Index